留学生实用汉语 99 例

主　编：张婧婧
副主编：张华清　张　妍

吉林大学出版社
·长春·

图书在版编目（CIP）数据

留学生实用汉语 99 例 / 张婧婧主编 .— 长春：吉林大学出版社，2021.10
ISBN 978-7-5692-9419-4

Ⅰ . ①留… Ⅱ . ①张… Ⅲ . ①汉语－对外汉语教学－教材 Ⅳ . ① H195.4

中国版本图书馆 CIP 数据核字（2021）第 223846 号

书　　名：	留学生实用汉语 99 例
	LIUXUESHENG SHIYONG HANYU 99 LI

作　　者：张婧婧　主编
策划编辑：邵宇彤
责任编辑：田　娜
责任校对：闫竞文
装帧设计：优盛文化
出版发行：吉林大学出版社
社　　址：长春市人民大街 4059 号
邮政编码：130021
发行电话：0431-89580028/29/21
网　　址：http://www.jlup.com.cn
电子邮箱：jdcbs@jlu.edu.cn
印　　刷：定州启航印刷有限公司
成品尺寸：170mm×240mm　　16 开
印　　张：12
字　　数：200 千字
版　　次：2021 年 10 月第 1 版
印　　次：2021 年 10 月第 1 次
书　　号：ISBN 978-7-5692-9419-4
定　　价：58.00 元

版权所有　　翻印必究

前　言
Preface

　　《留学生：实用汉语99例》是一本为拟在华留学、已在华留学、短期来华旅游生活以及汉语初级学习者编写的工具书，主要面向零起点汉语学习者以及掌握少量汉语词汇的初级水平汉语学习者。本书包括33个话题，涉及校园生活、饮食、购物、出行、生活娱乐五大实用主题。每个话题下设3个实用核心句子，3个实用场景，若干实用核心词汇，并提供必要的解释、实用技巧以及文化延伸。全书精选常用句型99例，99个实用场景和99个话题延伸，书中所选例句涉及日常生活中最简单、最真实的语句，具有实用性强、真实性强和针对性强的特点，希望能够帮助读者在短期内了解中国生活，学习生活必备语句，快速消除生活障碍，轻松融入中国生活。本书可以作为初级汉语教学内容的补充教材使用，也可作为短期速成汉语学习者的自学教材使用。

　　书中每个实用主题主要包含以下内容。

　　话题：每个主题细化为六七个不同的情境话题。例如"购物"这一主题就包含"逛菜场""逛超市""逛商场""网上购物""网上退换货""寄快递"6个子话题，几乎涵盖了购物的方方面面。

　　核心句子：每个话题列出和讲解了常见场合和情景中使用的3个核心句子，简单好用，并配以拼音和翻译，方便读者使用和理解。

　　实用情景：围绕核心句子，根据不同情景，设置对话，目的是帮助读者活用关键句，有效完成不同情境下的会话交流。

　　核心词汇：列出出现在对话中的词汇和与本主题相关的词汇，以供读者进行替换。

你知道吗：增补与主题密切相关的文化常识、实用技巧、生活窍门等拓展知识，让读者深刻理解话题。

为了方便回顾和查阅，本书最后还附有核心句子汇总表和核心词汇总表。使用本书学习的过程中，遇到不认识或不熟悉的单词或词组时，可以参看书后所附的词汇表。若想快速查找情境语句可以参看书后所附的句子汇总表。

目录
Contents

一、xiào yuán校 园 ······001

 wèn lù
 问 路 ······001

 shàng kè
 上 课 ······008

 kè chéng
 课 程 ······011

 wèn hòu
 问 候 ······015

 kǎo shì ān pái
 考试安排 ······018

 jié jià rì
 节假日 ······022

二、yǐn shí
饮 食 ······028

 qù nǎr chī fàn?
 去哪儿吃饭? ······028

 zài shí táng chī fàn
 在食堂吃饭 ······032

 zài fàn guǎn diǎn cài
 在饭馆点菜 ······035

 zài fàn guǎn fù qián
 在饭馆付钱 ······040

 dǎ bāo
 打 包 ······045

 diǎn wài mài
 点外卖 ······049

三、购物 ... 057

逛菜场 ... 057
逛超市 ... 061
逛商场 ... 066
网上购物 ... 070
网上退换货 ... 075
寄快递 ... 080

四、出行 ... 084

坐公交车 ... 084
坐出租车 ... 088
坐地铁 ... 092
坐高铁 ... 096
坐飞机 ... 101
订酒店房间 ... 105
入住酒店 ... 109

五、生活娱乐 ········· 114

看电影 ········· 114

去银行 ········· 118

租房 ········· 124

办理无线网络 ········· 129

去医院 ········· 134

微信 ········· 139

视频网站 ········· 145

过春节 ········· 150

附录 ········· 156

一、校园
Campus

问路
Asking the way

> 核心句子 （Kernel Sentence）

1. 请问，您知道教学楼怎么走吗？

Excuse me, do you know how to get to the teaching building?

在上课之前，您需要知道教学楼在什么地方，这样上课的时候才不会迷路。"请问"是一种礼貌用语，也可以换成"你好""打扰一下""不好意思"。"教学楼"可以换成"教室""超市""宿舍"等地名。

Before class, you need to know where the building is, so that you don't get lost during class. "qǐng wèn"(excuse me)is a polite expression. It can also be replaced with "nǐ hǎo""dǎ rǎo yī xià""bù hǎo yì si"(Hello, Excuse me and Sorry). "jiào xué lóu"(teaching building)can be replaced by"jiào shì""chāo shì""sù shè"("classroom", supermarket and dormitory)and other place names.

请问，您知道逸夫楼205教室怎么走吗？

Excuse me, do you know how to get to Room 205 of Yifu Building?

qǐng wèn, nín zhī dào fù jìn de chāo shì zěn me zǒu ma?
请问，您知道附近的超市怎么走吗？

Excuse me, do you know the way to the supermarket nearby?

nín kě yǐ bāng wǒ huà yì zhāng dì tú ma?
2. 您可以帮我画一张地图吗？

Can you draw a map for me?

当你需要别人给你提供某个地方的具体路线时，可以这样说。当然你得自己有笔和纸。

This is used when you need someone to give you a specific route to a place. Of course you have to have your own pen and paper.

yán zhe zhè tiáo lù yì zhí wǎng qián zǒu, dào le dì èr gè lù kǒu wǎng yòu guǎi.
3. 沿着这条路一直往前走，到了第二个路口往右拐。

Go straight along this road and turn right at the second crossing.

指路时经常会用到"左拐""右拐""往前走""东边""西边""北边""南边""旁边"，这些都表示行动的方向。

"zuǒ guǎi" "yòu guǎi" "wǎng qián zǒu" "dōng biān" "xī biān" "běi biān" "nán biān" "páng biān" (turning left, turning right, walking forward, east, west, north, south and side) are often used to guide the way, all of which indicate the direction of action.

☞ 实用场景（The Practical Situation）

bàn gōng shì zěn me zǒu?
» 1. 办公室怎么走？ Where is the office?

qǐng wèn, liú xué shēng bàn gōng shì zěn me zǒu?
A：请问，留学生办公室怎么走？

Excuse me, how can I get to the international students' office?

一、校　园

B：zài yì fū lóu 2 0 5 .
在逸夫楼２０５。

It's in Room 205, Yifu Building.

A：lí zhè lǐ yuǎn ma ?
离这里远吗？

Is it far from here?

B：bú tài yuǎn, yán zhe zhè tiáo lù yì zhí wǎng qián zǒu, dào le dì èr gè lù kǒu wǎng yòu guǎi .
不太远，沿着这条路一直往前走，到了第二个路口往右拐。

It's not too far. Go straight along this road and turn right at the second crossing.

A：nǐ néng bāng wǒ huà yì zhāng dì tú ma ?
你能帮我画一张地图吗？

Can you draw a map for me?

B：hǎo de .
好的。

OK.

» 2．nǐ qù nǎr ?你去哪儿？ Where are you going？

A：nǐ qù nǎr ?
你去哪儿？

Where are you going?

B：wǒ huí sù shè . nǐ qù nǎr ?
我回宿舍。你去哪儿？

I go back to my dorm. Where are you going?

A：wǒ qù xué xiào dà mén .
我去学校大门。

I go to the school gate.

·003·

nà wǒ men yì qǐ zǒu ba！
B：那 我 们 一 起 走 吧！

Let's go together then!

核心词汇（Key Words）

序号	词语	拼音	翻译
1	留学生	liú xué shēng	international students
2	办公室	bàn gōng shì	office
3	离	lí	from
4	一直	yì zhí	straight forward
5	往前	wǎng qián	forward
6	路口	lù kǒu	crossroads
7	右拐	yòu guǎi	turn right
8	地图	dì tú	map
9	宿舍	sù shè	dormitory
10	图书馆	tú shū guǎn	library
11	大门	dà mén	gate

你知道吗？——怎么使用共享单车？（Do you know？——How to use the bike-sharing？）

"Hellobike"，它的中文名叫"哈啰单车"，你可以在支付宝上直接使用，非常方便。具体的使用步骤如下。

Hellobike, it's called "hā luó dān chē" in Chinese. You can use it directly on Alipay, which is very convenient. The specific use steps are as follows.

第一，打开支付宝，找到"哈啰出行"，点击"进入"。

First, open Alipay, find "Hello Trip", and click "Enter".

一、校　园

第二，点击"扫一扫"。

Second, click "sǎo yi sǎo (scan)".

第三，对着车上的二维码扫描。

Third, scan the QR code on the bike.

留学生实用汉语99例

第四，点击"确认开锁"。

Fourth, click "què rèn kāi suǒ（Confirm to unlock）".

第五，骑行结束后，大家将哈啰单车停在自行车停放区域，再次扫描二维码，点击"我要还车"。然后用手把车锁关上，这时候会听到语音提示，最后选择支付即可。

Fifth, after riding, you should park your Hellobike in the bicycle parking area, scan the QR code again, and click "wǒ yào huán chē"(I want to return the bike).Then close the lock by hand, then you will hear the voice prompt, and finally choose to pay.

一、校　园

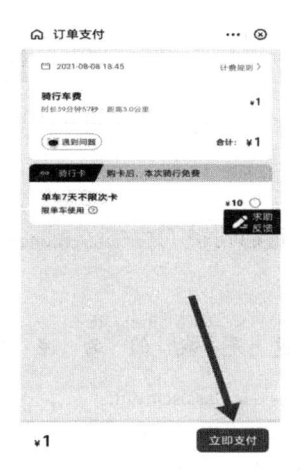

　　哈啰单车只能在运营区内骑行、停放。地图上蓝色区域为车辆运营区。当车辆在运营区外关锁，用户将被收取除车费外最高20元/单的车辆管理费。一些区域禁止停放共享单车，该区域即为禁停区。地图上红色区域为车辆禁停区。如车辆在禁停区内关锁，用户将被收取除车费外最高50元/单的车辆管理费。哈啰单车收费标准是1.5元/30分钟，不足30分钟，按照30分钟计算。

——参照支付宝"哈啰出行"里的"学习骑行规则"

　　Hellobike can only be ridden and parked in the operation area. The blue area on the map is the vehicle operation area. When the vehicle is locked outside the operation area, the user will be charged a vehicle management fee of up to 20 *yuan*/bill in addition to the fare. Some areas are forbidden to park bike-sharing, and this area is the forbidden zone. The red area on the map is the no-parking area for vehicles. If the vehicle is locked in the no-parking area, the user will be charged a vehicle management fee of up to 50 *yuan*/bill in addition to the fare. Hellobike charge standard is 1.5 *yuan*/30 minutes, less than 30 minutes, calculated according to 30 minutes.

shàng kè
上 课
Having Classes

核心句子（Kernel Sentence）

1. zhè shì wǒ men de kè biǎo.
   这 是 我 们 的 课 表。

   This is our class schedule.

   一般来说，课程任务和学时安排都是固定的。留学生上课也是根据课程类型来安排相应的学时和教学任务的。无特殊情况，一般不会更改和调换学时。

   In general, course assignments and class schedules are fixed. The class hours and teaching tasks for international students are also arranged according to the type of courses. The class hours will not be changed.

2. nǐ měi tiān yǒu duō shǎo jié kè?
   你 每 天 有 多 少 节 课？

   How many classes do you have every day?

   留学生的上课时间安排得很满，每天都有六节课，从早上8点开始。

   International students have a full schedule of classes. There are six classes every day, starting at 8:00 am.

3. wǒ men bú yào chí dào le.
   我 们 不 要 迟 到 了。

   Don't be late.

   中国老师会提前到教室进行课前准备，在课堂上也有一套完整的管理学生的办法，如班级规约等，会有固定时间安排学生讨论或小组活动，比较有纪律性。

一、校　园

Chinese teachers will go to the classroom in advance to prepare for class. In the classroom, they also have a complete set of measures to manage students, such as class regulations. They will have fixed time for students to discuss or to conduct group activities, which is more disciplined.

☞ 实用场景（The Practical Situation）

» 1. 询问上课时间　Asking about class time

A：wǒ men de shàng kè shí jiān shì zěn me ān pái de ?
　　我们的上课时间是怎么安排的？

What are our class hours?

B：měi tiān shàng wǔ　8:00-11:40，xià wǔ　2:00-5:40．
　　每天上午 8:00—11:40，下午 2:00—5:40。

Starting at 8:00 to 11:40 in the morning and 2:00 to 5:40 in the afternoon every day．

A：nǐ měi tiān yǒu duō shǎo jié kè ?
　　你每天有多少节课？

How many classes do you have every day?

B：wǒ měi tiān bù yí yàng, yǒu de shí hou 4 jié, yǒu de shí hou 6 jié．
　　我每天不一样，有的时候 4 节，有的时候 6 节。

My courses are all different．Sometimes I have four, sometimes I have six.

» 2. 不要迟到　Don't be late

A：nǐ jīn tiān zài nǎr shàng kè ?
　　你今天在哪儿上课？

Where do you have class today?

B：wǒ zài F 2 0 5，nǐ ne ?
　　我在 F205，你呢？

I'm in classroom F205. What about you?

· 009 ·

A：<ruby>我<rt>wǒ</rt></ruby> <ruby>在<rt>zài</rt></ruby> F201。<ruby>快<rt>kuài</rt></ruby><ruby>一<rt>yì</rt></ruby><ruby>点<rt>diǎn</rt></ruby><ruby>吧<rt>ba</rt></ruby>，<ruby>已<rt>yǐ</rt></ruby><ruby>经<rt>jīng</rt></ruby> 7:50 <ruby>了<rt>le</rt></ruby>，<ruby>马<rt>mǎ</rt></ruby><ruby>上<rt>shàng</rt></ruby><ruby>就<rt>jiù</rt></ruby><ruby>要<rt>yào</rt></ruby><ruby>上<rt>shàng</rt></ruby><ruby>课<rt>kè</rt></ruby><ruby>了<rt>le</rt></ruby>，<ruby>我<rt>wǒ</rt></ruby><ruby>们<rt>men</rt></ruby><ruby>不<rt>bú</rt></ruby><ruby>要<rt>yào</rt></ruby><ruby>迟<rt>chí</rt></ruby><ruby>到<rt>dào</rt></ruby><ruby>了<rt>le</rt></ruby>。

I'm in classroom F201. Hurry up! It's already 7:50, class is about to begin. Let's not be late.

B：<ruby>好<rt>hǎo</rt></ruby><ruby>的<rt>de</rt></ruby>，<ruby>走<rt>zǒu</rt></ruby><ruby>吧<rt>ba</rt></ruby>。

All right, let's go.

核心词汇（Key Words）

序号	词语	拼音	翻译
1	时间	shí jiān	time
2	安排	ān pái	to arrange
3	上午	shàng wǔ	morning
4	下午	xià wǔ	afternoon
5	节	jié	section
6	马上	mǎ shàng	immediately
7	迟到	chí dào	late

你知道吗？—— 中国学校的休学和退学（Do you know?—— Suspension of Schooling and dropping out of school in Chinese schools）

留学生应按照学校规定的课程表上课，不得无故请假或旷课。如因事、因病需请假，应按学校的规定办理。连续请假两个月以上，不能跟班学习者，作休学或留级处理。休学者保留学籍一年。无故旷课，按学校规定受校纪处分，情节严重的，令其退学。

——参考《外国留学生来华学习的有关规定》

International students should attend classes in accordance with the curriculum prescribed by the school, and should not ask for leave or absenteeism without any reason. If you need to take time off due to business or illness, it shall be handled according to the regulations of the school. Leave for more than two months in a row, and those who can't follow the classes will be suspended or repeated. Those who suspend schooling will be kept their student status for one year. If the student is absent from school without any reason, he/she will be punished according to the regulations of the school, and if the circumstances are serious, he/she will be ordered to drop out of school.

kè chéng
课 程
Courses

☞ 核心句子（Kernel Sentence）

nǐ yī gòng yǒu duō shǎo mén hàn yǔ kè ?
1. 你 一 共 有 多 少 门 汉 语 课 ?

How many Chinese courses do you have altogether?

"门"可以是名词，意为"door"。在这里，"门"是一个量词，如"一门课"，用在数词和名词之间。

"mén" can be a noun, it means "door". But in this case, "mén" is a quantifier, like "yì mén kè". It is used between a numeral and a noun.

zhāng lǎo shī duì wǒ men fēi cháng yán gé .
2. 张 老 师 对 我 们 非 常 严 格 。

Mr. Zhang is very strict with us.

中国有句古话"严师出高徒"，意思是：严格的好师傅或好老师，能教出本领高超的好徒弟或好学生。

There is an old Chinese saying that "a strict teacher produces outstanding students", which means that a strict good master or teacher can teach a good apprentice or student with excellent skills.

　　　　　měi tiān xià kè dōu bù zhì zuò yè．
3．每 天 下 课 都 布 置 作 业。

Homework is assigned every day after class.

作业是巩固教学效果的有力手段，也是反馈教学效果的重要途径之一，它不仅可以加深学生对基础知识的理解，而且有助于形成熟练的技能和发展学生的思维能力，是教学过程中不可缺少的重要环节，也是学生学习过程中一个重要组成部分。

Homework is not only a powerful means to consolidate teaching effect, but also an important way to feed back teaching effect. It can not only deepen students' understanding of basic knowledge, but also help to form skilled skills and develop students' thinking ability. It is an indispensable link in the teaching process and an important part of students' learning process.

☞ 实用场景（The Practical Situation）

» 1. 询问课程类型 Asking about course types

　　zuì jìn máng ma ?
A：最 近 忙 吗？

Are you busy lately?

　　yǒu diǎn máng, wǒ zhèng zài xué xí hàn yǔ．
B：有 点 忙， 我 正 在 学 习 汉 语。

A little busy. I'm learning Chinese.

　　nǐ yí gòng yǒu duō shǎo mén hàn yǔ kè ?
A：你 一 共 有 多 少 门 汉 语 课？

How many Chinese courses do you have altogether?

B：综合课、听力课、口语课。

Comprehensive class, listening class and speaking class.

» 2. 询问老师 Asking about the teacher

A：你们的综合课老师是张老师吗？

Is Mr. Zhang your comprehensive class teacher?

B：不是的，是李老师。

No, it's Miss Li.

A：李老师对你们严格吗？张老师对我们非常严格。

Is Miss Li strict with you? Mr. Zhang is very strict with us.

B：李老师对我们也很严格，每天下课都布置作业，上课检查作业，还纠正我们的发音。

Miss Li is very strict with us. She assigns homework after class every day. She checks homework in class and corrects our pronunciation.

A：看来老师们都很严格。

It seems that the teachers are all very strict.

核心词汇（Key Words）

序号	词语	拼音	翻译
1	最近	zuì jìn	recently
2	忙	máng	busy

续 表

3	门	mén	measure word
4	综合课	zōng hé kè	comprehensive course
5	听力课	tīng lì kè	listening course
6	口语课	kǒu yǔ kè	oral course
7	写作课	xiě zuò kè	writing course
8	阅读课	yuè dú kè	reading course
9	严格	yán gé	strict
10	纠正	jiū zhèng	to correct
11	发音	fā yīn	pronunciation

你知道吗?——外国留学生来中国的基础汉语学习要求
(Do you know?——Basic Chinese learning requirements for foreign students coming to China)

　　来华前未学过汉语或汉语水平达不到专业学习要求者,来华后需要学习一至二年基础汉语。其中:学习中国语言文学、历史、哲学、艺术史及中医等专业的本科生,需先学习两年基础汉语;学习理、工科及其他专业的本科生和进修生,需学习一年基础汉语。学习后,经考试汉语水平达到规定标准后,方可进入专业学习。

——参考《外国留学生来华学习的有关规定》

　　Those who have not learned Chinese before coming to China or whose Chinese level cannot meet the professional learning requirements need to study basic Chinese for one to two years after coming to China. Among them: Undergraduates studying Chinese language and literature, history, philosophy, art history and traditional Chinese medicine need to study basic Chinese for two years first; Undergraduates and advanced students studying science, engineering and other majors need to study basic Chinese for one year. After studying basic Chinese, you can start professional study only when your Chinese level has reached the prescribed standard after the examination.

一、校　园

问候
Greetings

> **核心句子**（Kernel Sentence）

1. 请问你（您）叫什么名字？
qǐng wèn nǐ (nín) jiào shén me míng zi?

What's your name, please?

中国人初次见面时，一般会礼貌地询问对方的姓名。"您"是"你"的尊敬说法，表示对对方的尊敬。中国人的姓名由姓和名组成，姓在前，名在后。

When Chinese people meet for the first time, they will politely ask for their names. "nín" is a respectful way of saying "nǐ", it's a sign of respect for others. Chinese names are made up of the surname and the given name, with the surname first and the given name second.

2. 我是韩国人。
wǒ shì hán guó rén.

I'm Korean.

表达国籍，一般都是"国名"+"人"，如"日本人""美国人"。

It is generally used to express the nationality by "country name" + "person", such as "rì běn rén" (Japanese), "měi guó rén" (American).

3. 你（您）好。
nǐ (nín) hǎo.

How do you do？/Hello.

看到或者遇到某人,可以用"你好"打招呼。如果是在早上,也可以说"早上好"。

You can say "hello" when you see or meet someone. If it's in the morning, you can also say "good morning".

实用场景(The Practical Situation)

» 1. 问姓名 Asking about the name

A:你好,我是张老师,请问你叫什么名字?
nǐ hǎo, wǒ shì zhāng lǎo shī, qǐng wèn nǐ jiào shén me míng zi?

Hello, I'm Miss Zhang. What's your name, please?

B:我叫Mike。
wǒ jiào Mike.

My name is Mike.

A:你有中文名字吗?
nǐ yǒu zhōng wén míng zi ma?

Do you have a Chinese name?

B:没有。
méi yǒu.

No.

» 2. 问国籍 Asking about the nationality

A:请问你是哪国人?
qǐng wèn nǐ shì nǎ guó rén?

What's your nationality, please?

B:我是日本人。
wǒ shì rì běn rén.

I'm Japanese.

一、校　园

A：nǐ hǎo, wǒ shì hán guó rén.
　　你好，我是韩国人。

　　Hello, I'm Korean.

B：nǐ hǎo.
　　你好。

　　Hello.

» 3. 问好 Say hello

A：xiǎo wáng, chū mén ya?
　　小王，出门呀？

　　Are you going out, Xiao Wang?

B：shì de. wǒ yào qù chāo shì mǎi dōng xi.
　　是的。我要去超市买东西。

　　Yes. I'm going to the supermarket to do some shopping.

核心词汇（Key Words）

序号	词语	拼音	翻译
1	名字	míng zi	name
2	你好	nǐ hǎo	hello
3	叫	jiào	to call
4	国家	guó jiā	country
5	超市	chāo shì	supermarket
6	韩国	hán guó	Republic of Korea
7	美国	měi guó	United States
8	日本	rì běn	Japan

留学生实用汉语99例

> ☞ **你知道吗？—— 中国人怎么打招呼？**（Do you know?——How do Chinese people say hello？）

在中国，与陌生人初次见面，人们会说："你（您）好""大家好"等，并礼貌询问对方姓名、职业等。当我们与朋友见面问候时，一般常常问一些日常生活上的事情。比如，吃饭的时候遇见了，你会说"吃过了吗？"；出门的时候遇见了，你会说"出门呀？"。这些问话都是像"你好"一样在打招呼，并不是真的在提问。

In China, when you meet a stranger for the first time, you will say, "nǐ(nín)hǎo""dà jiā hǎo", and so on. And at the same time, you can ask the person's name and occupation politely. When we meet and greet our friends, we often ask about things in daily life. For example, if you meet someone at dinner, you will say "Have you eaten yet?"; When you meet someone on the way out, you will say "Are you going out?".These questions are greetings like "Hello". They are not really asking questions.

kǎo shì ān pái
考试安排
Exam arrangement

> ☞ **核心句子**（Kernel Sentence）

qǐngwèn, tīng lì kè shén me shí hou kǎo shì ?
1. 请问，听力课什么时候考试？

Excuse me, when is the listening test?

在大学，考试大概需要一周甚至两周的时间，在这一两周内，所有专业不上课，有部分专业举行考试。考试一般都是间隔两三天考一门。

In college, the exam takes about a week or even two weeks. In this week or two, there are no classes for all majors, and some majors hold exams. Exams are usually two or three days apart.

2. 期末考试是闭卷考试，请大家遵守考试纪律。
qī mò kǎo shì shì bì juàn kǎo shì, qǐng dà jiā zūn shǒu kǎo shì jì lǜ.

The final exam is a closed-book exam. Please observe the discipline of the examination.

闭卷考试是考试的一种类型。考生只可以独立完成试题，不可以看课本和资料，不可以与其他考生商量答案、传答案等，否则计0分。

Closed-book examination is a type of examination. Examinees can only complete the examination questions independently, do not read textbooks and materials, and do not discuss and pass on answers with other examinees, otherwise 0 points will be counted.

3. 期末考试考得怎么样？
qī mò kǎo shì kǎo de zěn me yàng?

How is your final exam?

百分数制是学校评定学生成绩的一种计分方法。一百分为最高成绩，六十分为及格。

The percentage system is a method of scoring for schools to assess students' achievements. One hundred is the highest score, and sixty is a passing grade.

实用场景（The Practical Situation）

» 1. 询问考试 Asking about the exam

A：李老师，请问听力课什么时候考试？
lǐ lǎo shī, qǐng wèn tīng lì kè shén me shí hou kǎo shì?

Miss Li, when is the listening test?

B：下周二下午5、6节课考试。
xià zhōu èr xià wǔ 5、6 jié kè kǎo shì.

The exam will be in the fifth and sixth classes next Tuesday afternoon.

A：kǎo shì nán ma?
考试难吗?

Was the exam difficult?

B：kǎo shì bù nán, zhǐ yào hǎo hǎo fù xí jiù kě yǐ dé gāo fēn.
考试不难,只要好好复习就可以得高分。

The exam is not difficult. You can get a high mark as long as you review well.

» 2. 询问考试纪律 Asking about exam discipline

A：lǐ lǎo shī, qī mò kǎo shì shí kě yǐ kàn shǒu jī ma?
李老师,期末考试时可以看手机吗?

Miss Li, can I look through my phone during the final exam?

B：dāng rán bù xíng. qī mò kǎo shì shì bì juàn kǎo shì, qǐng dà jiā zūn shǒu kǎo shì jì lǜ.
当然不行。期末考试是闭卷考试,请大家遵守考试纪律。

Of course not. The final exam is a closed-book exam, so please observe the discipline.

» 3. 询问考试成绩 Asking about test results

A：nǐ qī mò kǎo shì kǎo de zěn me yàng?
你期末考试考得怎么样?

How did you do on your final exam?

B：bú tài hǎo. tè bié shì tīng lì kǎo shì, zhǐ dé le 75 fēn. nǐ ne?
不太好。特别是听力考试,只得了75分。你呢?

Not so good, especially on the listening test. I only got 75. How about you?

A：wǒ kǎo de yě bú tài hǎo, zōng hé kè zhǐ dé le 70 fēn. bú guò tīng lì kǎo de hái kě yǐ.
我考得也不太好,综合课只得了70分。不过听力考得还可以。

I didn't do very well either. I only got 70 on the comprehensive course, but I did OK on the listening test.

一、校 园

核心词汇（Key Words）

序 号	词 语	拼 音	翻 译
1	考试	kǎo shì	test
2	周二	zhōu èr	Tuesday
3	难	nán	difficult
4	复习	fù xí	to review
5	纪律	jì lǜ	discipline
6	怎么样	zěn me yàng	How's that
7	还可以	hái kě yǐ	not bad
8	不太好	bú tài hǎo	not so well

你知道吗？——汉语水平考试（HSK）[Do you know?——Chinese Proficiency Test（HSK）]

汉语水平考试（HSK）是依据《国际汉语能力标准》《HSK考试大纲》组织实施的一项国际标准化考试，重点考查汉语非第一语言的考生在生活、学习和工作中运用汉语进行交际的能力。HSK考试有6个级别，其成绩是外国学生来华留学、申请奖学金的必备条件；是外国人来华工作、申请永久居留、移民等的语言证明，并被越来越多的跨国企业作为员工招聘和晋升的重要依据。

——参考中外语言交流合作中心官网（网址:www.chinesetest.cn。）

The HSK examines the ability of non-native speakers to communicate in Chinese in their daily life, study and work in accordance with *the Chinese Language Proficiency Scales for Speakers of Other Languages* and *the HSK Test Syllabi*. The Test consists of six levels, serving as a prerequisite for foreign students to study in China and to apply for scholarships; for foreigners to work in China, apply for permanent residence, immigration, etc. It is also widely used by multinational enterprises as a key basis for recruitment and promotion.

节假日
On vacation

> **核心句子**（Kernel Sentence）

1. 中秋节就要到了，我们要放三天假。

The Mid-Autumn Festival is coming, we will have a three-day holiday.

每年农历八月十五是中国的中秋节。中秋节又称祭月节、拜月节、团圆节等，是中国民间的传统节日。中秋节自古便有祭月、赏月、吃月饼、玩花灯、赏桂花、饮桂花酒等民俗，流传至今，经久不息。中秋节以月之圆预兆人之团圆，为寄托思念故乡、思念亲人之情，祈盼丰收、幸福，成为丰富多彩、弥足珍贵的文化遗产。中秋节与春节、清明节、端午节并称为中国四大传统节日。受中华文化的影响，中秋节也是东亚和东南亚一些国家尤其是当地的华人华侨的传统节日。2006年5月20日，国务院将其列入首批国家级非物质文化遗产名录。自2008年起中秋节被列为国家法定节假日。

——参考360百科"中秋节"https://baike.so.com/doc/2427843-2566655.html

The Mid-Autumn Festival in China falls on the 15th day of the eighth lunar month every year. Mid-Autumn Festival, also known as Moon Festival, Reunion Festival, is a traditional Chinese folk festival. Since ancient times, Mid-Autumn Festival has had folk customs such as offering sacrifices to the moon, enjoying the moon, eating moon cakes, playing with lanterns, enjoying sweet-scented osmanthus, and drinking osmanthus wine, which have been passed down to this day and lasted for a long time. Mid-Autumn Festival heralds people's reunion with the full moon, cherishes the feelings of missing hometown and relatives, and prays for a bumper harvest and happiness, thus becoming a colorful and precious cultural heritage. Mid-Autumn Festival, Spring Festival, Tomb-Sweeping Day and Dragon Boat Festival are called the four traditional festivals in

一、校　园

China. Influenced by Chinese culture, Mid-Autumn Festival is also a traditional festival for some countries in East and Southeast Asia, especially local Chinese and overseas Chinese. On May 20, 2006, the State Council listed it in the first batch of National Intangible Cultural Heritage. Mid-Autumn Festival has been listed as a national legal holiday since 2008.

2. 除了暑假、寒假，还有其他很多假期。
   chú le shǔ jià、hán jià, hái yǒu qí tā hěn duō jià qī.

There are many other holidays besides summer vacation and winter vacation.

人们经常把节日与假日相混淆，事实上大多数节日都没有法定假期。例如，中国传统节日重阳节、寒食节都没有假期。

People often confuse festivals with holidays. In fact, most festivals have no statutory holidays. For example, Chinese traditional festivals such as Double Ninth Festival and Cold Food Festival have no holidays.

3. 我们什么时候放寒假？
   wǒ men shén me shí hou fàng hán jià?

When is the winter holiday?

只有学校才有寒暑假，寒假一般是从农历腊月初十左右开始，元宵节后寒假结束。在寒假期间有我们最重大的节日——春节。

Only schools have winter and summer vacations. Winter vacation generally begins at about the tenth day of the twelfth lunar month and ends after the Lantern Festival. During the winter vacation, there is our most important festival, Spring Festival.

☞ 实用场景（The Practical Situation）

» 1. 中秋节 Mid-Autumn Festival

A：中秋节就要到了，我们要放三天假。
   zhōng qiū jié jiù yào dào le, wǒ men yào fàng sān tiān jià.

The Mid-Autumn Festival is coming, we will have a three-day holiday.

· 023 ·

B：真的吗？

Really?

A：是的，李老师刚刚说的。

Yes, Miss Li just said it.

B：中秋节放假我们做什么呢？

What shall we do on the Mid-Autumn Festival holiday?

A：我们去参加学院组织的中秋晚会吧，可以看节目还可以吃月饼。

Let's attend the Mid-Autumn Festival party organized by the college. We can watch the programs and eat moon cakes.

» 2. 中国传统节日 Chinese traditional festival

A：今天是我们国家的农耕节，一个非常重要的节日。

Today is our country's Agricultural Festival, a very important festival.

B：哦，是为了祈祷风调雨顺五谷丰登吗？

Oh, is it to pray for good weather and good harvests?

A：对呀。中国除了暑假、寒假，还有其他的假期吗？

That's right. Are there any other holidays besides summer vacation and winter vacation in China?

B：当然有呀。中国的很多节日都源于传统习俗。例如，春节、中秋节、清明节、重阳节等等。

Of course there is. Many festivals in China originate from traditional customs, such as Spring Festival, Mid-Autumn Festival, Tomb-Sweeping Day, Double Ninth Festival and so on.

A：这些节日都放假吗？

Are all these festivals off?

B：有的放假，有的不放假。

Some have holidays, some don't.

3. 放寒假 Winter vacation

A：我们什么时候放寒假呀？我想提前预订回国的飞机票。

When shall we have winter vacation? I'd like to book a flight back home in advance.

B：按照校历算应该下周就要考试吧。考完试应该就要放假了。

According to the school calendar, the exam should be held next week. There should be a holiday after the exam.

A：哦，那我就预订下下周的飞机票吧。

Oh, I'll book a flight for the week after next.

wǒ jué de nǐ hái shi wèn wèn lǎo shī bǐ jiào hǎo.
B：我 觉 得 你 还 是 问 问 老 师 比 较 好。

I think you'd better ask the teacher.

☞ 核心词汇（Key Words）

序号	词语	拼音	翻译
1	节日	jié rì	holiday
2	暑假	shǔ jià	summer vacation
3	寒假	hán jià	winter vacation
4	春节	chūn jié	Spring Festival
5	元宵节	yuán xiāo jié	Lantern Festival
6	清明节	qīng míng jié	Qingming Festival
7	端午节	duān wǔ jié	Dragon Boat Festival
8	重阳节	chóng yáng jié	Double Ninth Festival
9	中秋节	zhōng qiū jié	Mid-Autumn Festival
10	国庆节	guó qìng jié	National Day
11	月饼	yuè bing	moon cake
12	汤圆	tāng yuán	sweet soup balls
13	粽子	zòng zi	Zongzi

☞ 你知道吗？—— 中国的假期（Do you know?—— Holidays in China）

假期是指国家法定的假日，也指单位规定的休假日。除双休日外，我国国定假期为元旦、春节、清明、劳动节、端午、中秋、国庆。在中国，学校通常将每个学年分为上、下两个学期。上学期从秋季八月中旬或九月初开始，到第二年的一月底左右结束。此时各学校开始放假，而这个假期正处于中国寒冷的冬季，就称为寒假，寒假一般正月十五结束。下学期从

一、校　园

春季二月中旬开始，到七月初或七月中旬结束，各学校又开始放假，而这个假期正处于中国最炎热的夏季，就称为暑假。

——参考360百科"假期"https://baike.so.com/doc/5341774-5577217.html

  Holiday refers to the national statutory holiday, also refers to the unit's holiday. Except weekends, the national holidays in China are New Year's Day, Spring Festival, Qingming Festival, Labor Day, Dragon Boat Festival, Mid-Autumn Festival and National Day. In China, schools usually divide each academic year into two semesters. The first semester begins in mid-August or early September in autumn and ends at the end of January of the following year. At this time, schools begin to have a holiday, and this holiday is in the cold winter in China, which is called winter vacation, which usually ends on the fifteenth day of the first lunar month. The next semester starts in mid-February in spring and ends in early July or mid-July, and schools start to have holidays again. This holiday is in the hottest summer in China, which is called summer vacation.

二、饮食 (yǐn shí)
Diet

去哪儿吃饭？(qù nǎr chī fàn?)
Where shall we eat?

> **核心句子**（Kernel Sentence）

1. 你去哪儿吃饭？ (nǐ qù nǎr chī fàn?)

Where do you want to eat?

如果说话人和听话人要一起去吃饭，可以改为"我们去哪儿吃饭"，询问对方意见。

If the speaker and the listener are going to eat together, you can change it to "wǒ men qù nǎr chī fàn?"(Where shall we eat?). It is used to ask for advice.

2. 我们去万达吃饭怎么样？ (wǒ men qù wàn dá chī fàn zěn me yàng?)

Shall we go to Wanda for dinner?

"怎么样"放在句子末尾可以询问状况或者意见。

Put "zěn me yàng" at the end of a sentence to ask for status or advice.

3. 你想吃什么？ (nǐ xiǎng chī shén me?)

What would you want to eat?

二、饮　食

☞ 实用场景（The Practical Situation）

» 1. 中午去哪儿吃饭？ Where are you going for lunch?

A：dà wèi, nǐ zhōng wǔ qù nǎr chī fàn？
　　大卫，你中午去哪儿吃饭？

David, where are you going for lunch?

B：wǒ yě bù zhī dào qù nǎr chī fàn.
　　我也不知道去哪儿吃饭。

I don't know where to eat either.

A：wǒ men qù wàn dá chī fàn zěn me yàng？
　　我们去万达吃饭怎么样？

How about going to Wanda for dinner?

B：hǎo de, wǒ men yì qǐ qù ba.
　　好的，我们一起去吧。

OK, let's go together.

» 2. 你想吃什么？ What would you want to eat?

A：xià kè le, wǒ men kuài qù chī fàn ba.
　　下课了，我们快去吃饭吧。

Class is over. Let's go to have dinner.

B：hǎo de, nǐ xiǎng chī shén me？
　　好的，你想吃什么？

OK, what would you want to eat?

A：wǒ tài è le, shén me dōu xiǎng chī. nǐ ne？
　　我太饿了，什么都想吃。你呢？

I'm so hungry, anything is OK. How about you?

· 029 ·

wǒ huí sù shè zuò chǎomiàn.
B：我 回 宿 舍 做 炒 面。

I'm going back to my dorm to make fried noodles.

» 3. 谈论中国菜 Talking about the Chinese food

nǐ chī shén me ne? zhēnxiāng a!
A：你 吃 什 么 呢？真 香 啊！

What are you eating? It's so sweet!

wǒ zài chī mǐ fàn hé chǎo cài.
B：我 在 吃 米 饭 和 炒 菜。

I'm eating rice and stir-fry.

kàn qǐ lai zhēn bú cuò. hǎo chī ma?
A：看 起 来 真 不 错。好 吃 吗？

It looks really good. Does it taste good?

zhè ge shì yú xiāng ròu sī. hái bú cuò, suān suān là là de, jiù shì yóu
B：这 个 是 鱼 香 肉 丝。还 不 错，酸 酸 辣 辣 的，就 是 油
yǒu diǎn duō.
有 点 多。

This is shredded pork in fish-flavored sauce. It's not bad. It's sour and spicy, but a little oily.

ò, wǒ shàng cì mǎi de fān qié chǎo jī dàn yě hěn hǎo chī.
A：哦，我 上 次 买 的 番 茄 炒 鸡 蛋 也 很 好 吃。

Oh, and the scrambled egg with tomato I bought last time was delicious, too.

shì de, xué xiào shí táng de fàn cài tǐng hǎo chī de.
B：是 的，学 校 食 堂 的 饭 菜 挺 好 吃 的。

Yes, the food in the school cafeteria is delicious.

二、饮　食

☞ 核心词汇（Key Words）

序号	词语	拼音	翻译
1	吃饭	chī fàn	have a meal
2	炒面	chǎo miàn	fried noodles
3	米饭	mǐ fàn	rice
4	包子	bāo zi	steamed stuffed bun
5	豆浆	dòu jiāng	soybean milk
6	炒菜	chǎo cài	stir-fry dish
7	热干面	rè gān miàn	hot-and-dry noodles
8	饺子	jiǎo zi	dumplings
9	西红柿炒鸡蛋	xī hóng shì chǎo jī dàn	scrambled egg with tomato
10	鱼香肉丝	yú xiāng ròu sī	shredded pork in first-flavored sauce
11	糖醋里脊	táng cù lǐ ji	sweet and sour fillet of pork

☞ 你知道吗？—— 中国八大菜系（Do you know?—— Eight Chinese Cuisines）

　　中国饮食可以大致分为八大菜系，即鲁菜、川菜、粤菜、苏菜、闽菜、浙菜、湘菜、徽菜。这种分类已被广为接受。当然，还有其他很多著名的地方菜系，如北京菜和上海菜。

　　Generally, Chinese food can be roughly divided into eight regional cuisines, which has been widely accepted around. They are Shandong Cuisine, Sichuan Cuisine, Guangdong Cuisine, Jiangsu Cuisine, Fujian Cuisine, Zhejiang Cuisine, Hunan Cuisine, Anhui Cuisine.Certainly, there are many other local cuisines that are famous, such as Beijing Cuisine and Shanghai Cuisine.

在食堂吃饭
Eating in the canteen

> **核心句子**(Kernel Sentence)

1. 我要一个包子和一杯豆浆。

I want a steamed stuffed bun and a cup of soybean milk.

"要"在这里是动词,意为"希望得到"。"个""杯"都是量词。

"yào" here is a verb with the meaning "to wish for", "gè" and "bēi" are quantifiers.

2. 请把餐盘和垃圾带走,放到出口的餐盘回收处。

Please take your plates and garbage away and put them in the tray recycling area at the exit.

在学校食堂里吃饭,吃完以后,要把餐盘和垃圾带走,放到出口的餐盘回收处。

Eating in the school canteen, the plates and the garbage should be taken away and put in the plate recycling place at the exit.

3. 我要打包。

I want to pack the food.

I need a doggy bag.

"打"在这里是动词,意为捆;"包"这里也是动词,意为包装。"打包"的意思是用袋子装好食物。

"Dǎ" here is a verb. It means to bundle; "bāo" is also a verb. It means to wrap. "dǎ bāo" means to put food in a bag.

实用场景 (The Practical Situation)

» 1. 食堂怎么走？ Where is the canteen?

A: nǐ hǎo, qǐng wèn nǎ lǐ yǒu shí táng?
你好，请问哪里有食堂？

Excuse me, where is the canteen?

B: qián biān shì hé yuán shí táng, wǒ dài nǐ qù.
前边是荷园食堂，我带你去。

There is the Lotus Garden canteen. I'll show you.

A: zhè lǐ shí táng de jià qián zěn me yàng?
这里食堂的价钱怎么样？

What about the food price of the canteen here?

B: hé cān guǎn xiāng bǐ, zhè biān de jià qián pián yi yì diǎn, dàn shì wèi dào yì bān.
和餐馆相比，这边的价钱便宜一点，但是味道一般。

Compared to restaurants, the prices here are lower, but the taste is just so-so.

» 2. 在食堂吃饭 Eating in the cafeteria

A: nǐ hǎo, wǒ yào yí gè bāo zi hé yì bēi dòu jiāng.
你好，我要一个包子和一杯豆浆。

Hello, I'd like a steamed stuffed bun and a cup of soybean milk.

B: hǎo de, sān kuài wǔ, qǐng shuā kǎ.
好的，三块五，请刷卡。

OK, three *yuan* and a half, please swipe the card.

wǒ yào dǎ bāo
A：我要打包。

I want to pack the food.

hǎo de
B：好的。

Alright.

» 3. 吃完饭后 After eating

wǒ chī bǎo le
A：我吃饱了。

I'm full.

nǐ xū yào bǎ cān pán hé lā jī dài zǒu fàng dào chū kǒu de cān pán huí shōu chù
B：你需要把餐盘和垃圾带走放到出口的餐盘回收处。

You need to take your plates and trash away, and put them in the tray recycling area at the exit.

hǎo de, xiè xie
A：好的，谢谢！

OK, thank you.

☞ 核心词汇 (Key Words)

序号	词语	拼音	翻译
1	餐盘	cān pán	plate
2	垃圾	lā jī	garbage
3	回收处	huí shōu chù	recycling place
4	馒头	mán tou	steamed bread
5	饼	bǐng	pancake
6	西瓜汁	xī guā zhī	watermelon juice
7	价钱	jià qián	price

二、饮　食

续表

序号	词语	拼音	翻译
8	刷卡	shuā kǎ	to swipe card

☞ 你知道吗？—— 中国饮食四季有别（Do you know?—— Chinese food is different in four seasons）

一年四季，按季节而吃，是中国烹饪又一大特征。自古以来，中国一直按季节变化来调味、配菜，冬天味醇浓厚，夏天清淡凉爽；冬天多炖焖煨，夏天多凉拌冷冻。

——参考 360 百科"中国饮食文化"
https://baike.so.com/doc/5375680-31352160.html

Eating according to seasons all year round is another major feature of Chinese coOKing. Since ancient times, people have been seasoning and making side dishes in China according to seasonal changes, with strong flavor in winter and light in summer; Stewing more in winter and cold frozen dishes in summer.

在饭馆点菜
Ordering at a restaurant

☞ 核心句子（Kernel Sentence）

1. 请问您现在要点餐吗？
   qǐng wèn nín xiàn zài yào diǎn cān ma ?
   May I take your order now?

"点"在这里是动词,意为在许多事物中指定某个,如"点菜""点歌"。"餐"为名词,意思是饭菜。

"diǎn" is a verb here, which means to specify something in many things, such as "diǎn cài" (ordering) and "diǎn gē"(choosing songs). "cān" is a noun, which means food.

2．今天有什么特价菜吗？
jīn tiān yǒu shén me tè jià cài ma

Do you have any special today?

"特价"是名词,意思是特别低的价格,如"特价菜""特价商品"。

"tè jià" is a noun and it means a very low price, such as "tè jià cài"(special food) "tè jià shāng pǐn" (off-price merchandise).

3．点餐请扫码。
diǎn cān qǐng sǎo mǎ

Please scan the code to order.

"扫码"是用微信自带的"扫一扫"工具或其他二维码扫描工具,扫描餐厅的二维码,从而进行点餐的动作。现在很多吃饭的地方都使用点餐系统,不用服务员,也没有纸质菜单。

"sǎo mǎ" refers to the action of scanning the restaurant's QR code with the "Scan" tool or other QR code scanning tools, so as to order food. Nowadays, many places where people eat use the ordering system, without waiters or paper menus.

实用场景（The Practical Situation）

» 1. 特价菜 Special dishes

A：这是菜单，看看想吃点什么？
zhè shì cài dān, kàn kan xiǎng chī diǎn shén me

Here is the menu. What would you like to have?

二、饮食

B：今天有什么特价菜？
jīn tiān yǒu shén me tè jià cài ?

What's the special today?

A：东坡肉今天特价，只要20块一份。
dōng pō ròu jīn tiān tè jià, zhǐ yào 20 kuài yí fèn.

Dongpo pork is on sale today. It's only 20 *yuan* a piece.

B：好，那就来一份吧。
hǎo, nà jiù lái yí fèn ba.

OK, I'll have one.

2. 点餐 Order

A：先生，您现在要点餐吗？
xiānsheng, nín xiàn zài yào diǎn cān ma ?

Would you like to order now, Sir?

B：不好意思，我还没想好要吃什么。
bù hǎo yì si, wǒ hái méi xiǎng hǎo yào chī shén me.

I'm sorry, I haven't decided what to eat yet.

A：您有什么忌口的吗？
nín yǒu shén me jì kǒu de ma ?

Are there any foods you don't like?

B：没有。
méi yǒu.

No.

A：牛肉今天特价，味道很不错。
niú ròu jīn tiān tè jià, wèi dào hěn bú cuò.

The beef is on special today. It's very tasty.

· 037 ·

B：<ruby>好<rt>hǎo</rt></ruby>，<ruby>那<rt>nà</rt></ruby> <ruby>就<rt>jiù</rt></ruby> <ruby>来<rt>lái</rt></ruby> <ruby>一<rt>yí</rt></ruby> <ruby>份<rt>fèn</rt></ruby> <ruby>吧<rt>ba</rt></ruby>。

OK, I'll have one then.

» 3. 你喜欢吃什么？What do you like to eat?

A：<ruby>你<rt>nǐ</rt></ruby> <ruby>喜<rt>xǐ</rt></ruby> <ruby>欢<rt>huan</rt></ruby> <ruby>吃<rt>chī</rt></ruby> <ruby>什<rt>shén</rt></ruby> <ruby>么<rt>me</rt></ruby>？

What do you like to eat?

B：<ruby>都<rt>dōu</rt></ruby> <ruby>还<rt>hái</rt></ruby> <ruby>可<rt>kě</rt></ruby> <ruby>以<rt>yǐ</rt></ruby>。<ruby>最<rt>zuì</rt></ruby> <ruby>喜<rt>xǐ</rt></ruby> <ruby>欢<rt>huan</rt></ruby> <ruby>吃<rt>chī</rt></ruby> <ruby>酸<rt>suān</rt></ruby> <ruby>辣<rt>là</rt></ruby> <ruby>口<rt>kǒu</rt></ruby> <ruby>味<rt>wèi</rt></ruby> <ruby>的<rt>de</rt></ruby>。

Anything is OK. But I like sour and hot best.

A：<ruby>行<rt>xíng</rt></ruby>！<ruby>那<rt>nà</rt></ruby> <ruby>咱<rt>zán</rt></ruby> <ruby>们<rt>men</rt></ruby> <ruby>点<rt>diǎn</rt></ruby> <ruby>一<rt>yí</rt></ruby> <ruby>个<rt>gè</rt></ruby> <ruby>糖<rt>táng</rt></ruby> <ruby>醋<rt>cù</rt></ruby> <ruby>里<rt>lǐ</rt></ruby> <ruby>脊<rt>ji</rt></ruby> <ruby>或<rt>huò</rt></ruby> <ruby>者<rt>zhě</rt></ruby> <ruby>酸<rt>suān</rt></ruby> <ruby>菜<rt>cài</rt></ruby> <ruby>鱼<rt>yú</rt></ruby> <ruby>怎<rt>zěn</rt></ruby> <ruby>么<rt>me</rt></ruby> <ruby>样<rt>yàng</rt></ruby>？

Good! How about a sweet and sour pork or fish with sauerkraut?

B：<ruby>那<rt>nà</rt></ruby> <ruby>就<rt>jiù</rt></ruby> <ruby>酸<rt>suān</rt></ruby> <ruby>菜<rt>cài</rt></ruby> <ruby>鱼<rt>yú</rt></ruby> <ruby>吧<rt>ba</rt></ruby>。

Fish with sauerkraut, then.

A：<ruby>好<rt>hǎo</rt></ruby> <ruby>的<rt>de</rt></ruby>，<ruby>再<rt>zài</rt></ruby> <ruby>点<rt>diǎn</rt></ruby> <ruby>一<rt>yí</rt></ruby> <ruby>个<rt>gè</rt></ruby> <ruby>麻<rt>má</rt></ruby> <ruby>婆<rt>pó</rt></ruby> <ruby>豆<rt>dòu</rt></ruby> <ruby>腐<rt>fu</rt></ruby>、<ruby>一<rt>yí</rt></ruby> <ruby>个<rt>gè</rt></ruby> <ruby>东<rt>dōng</rt></ruby> <ruby>坡<rt>pō</rt></ruby> <ruby>肉<rt>ròu</rt></ruby> <ruby>和<rt>hé</rt></ruby> <ruby>一<rt>yí</rt></ruby> <ruby>个<rt>gè</rt></ruby> <ruby>炒<rt>chǎo</rt></ruby> <ruby>青<rt>qīng</rt></ruby> <ruby>菜<rt>cài</rt></ruby>。<ruby>喝<rt>hē</rt></ruby> <ruby>点<rt>diǎn</rt></ruby> <ruby>什<rt>shén</rt></ruby> <ruby>么<rt>me</rt></ruby> <ruby>呢<rt>ne</rt></ruby>？

OK, one Mapo Tofu, one Dongpo pork and one stir-fried green vegetables. Would you like something to drink?

B：<ruby>就<rt>jiù</rt></ruby> <ruby>喝<rt>hē</rt></ruby> <ruby>茶<rt>chá</rt></ruby> <ruby>吧<rt>ba</rt></ruby>。

Just tea.

二、饮　食

☞ 核心词汇（Key Words）

序号	词语	拼音	翻译
1	菜单	cài dān	menu
2	特价菜	tè jià cài	special
3	东坡肉	dōng pō ròu	Dongpo pork
4	酸菜鱼	suān cài yú	fish with sauerkraut
5	麻婆豆腐	má pó dòu fu	Mapo Tofu
6	点餐	diǎn cān	to order
7	忌口	jì kǒu	to avoid certain food
8	酸	suān	sour
9	辣	là	spicy
10	甜	tián	sweet
11	苦	kǔ	bitter

☞ 你知道吗？——东坡肉（Do you know?——Dongpo pork）

　　东坡肉是中国十大名菜之一。东坡肉一般是一块约 6 厘米左右的方正形猪肉，一半为肥肉，一半为瘦肉，入口香糯、肥而不腻，带有酒香，色泽红亮，味醇汁浓，酥烂而形不碎，十分美味。

　　Dongpo pork is one of the top ten famous dishes in China. Dongpo pork is usually a square piece of pork about six centimeters long, half of which is fat and half of which is lean. It is sweet and waxy, fat but not greasy, with wine aroma, bright red color, mellow and thick juice, crisp but not brOKen, and very delicious.

在饭馆付钱
zài fàn guǎn fù qián
Pay at a restaurant

核心句子（Kernel Sentence）

1. 服务员，买单。
   fú wù yuán, mǎi dān.

   Excuse me, bill please.

   "买单"是动词，意为结账付款。"买单"来源于粤语的"埋单"，传入北方地区后，大多数人都说成"买单"。

   "mǎi dān" is a verb, which means paying the bill. "mǎi dān" comes from the Cantonese word "mái dān". After it was introduced into the northern region, most people said "mǎi dān".

2. 今天我请客。
   jīn tiān wǒ qǐng kè.

   It's on me today.

   It's my treat today.

3. 您怎么付款？是用微信、支付宝还是现金？
   nín zěn me fù kuǎn? shì yòng wēi xìn、zhī fù bǎo hái shì xiàn jīn?

   How would you like to pay? WeChat, Alipay or cash?

   现今，在中国，我们在外面消费时很少直接用现金，大多用手机扫码支付。用户通过手机客户端扫二维码或商家使用电子支付工具扫描用户的付款码，便可实现与商家账户的支付结算。比较常见的支付方式就是微信、支付宝。

   Nowadays in China, when we spend money outside, we rarely use cash directly. We mostly pay by scanning the code on our mobile phones. The user scans the QR code via

二、饮　食

the mobile client or the merchant scans the user's payment code by using an electronic payment tool to achieve payment settlement with the merchant's account. The most common payment methods are WeChat and Alipay.

实用场景（The Practical Situation）

» 1. 付款方式 Payment method

A：您好！请问这顿饭多少钱？
　　nín hǎo! qǐng wèn zhè dùn fàn duō shǎo qián?

Hello! How much is the meal, please?

B：28 元。
　　2 8 yuán.

28 yuan.

A：好的。
　　hǎo de.

OK.

B：您怎么付款？是用微信、支付宝还是现金？
　　nín zěn me fù kuǎn? shì yòng wēi xìn、zhī fù bǎo hái shì xiàn jīn?

How would you like to pay? WeChat, Alipay or cash?

A：微信扫码。
　　wēi xìn sǎo mǎ.

WeChat.

B：付好了。请慢走。欢迎您下次再来。
　　fù hǎo le. qǐng màn zǒu. huān yíng nín xià cì zài lái.

It's OK. Take your time, please. You are welcome to come again.

· 041 ·

» 2. 结账 Check out

A：服务员，买单。
　　fú wù yuán, mǎi dān.

Excuse me, bill please.

B：好的，一共消费２６７元。
　　hǎo de, yí gòng xiāo fèi 2 6 7 yuán.

OK, that's 267 *yuan* in total.

A：可以微信扫码吗？
　　kě yǐ wēi xìn sǎo mǎ ma?

Can I scan the code on WeChat?

B：可以。
　　kě yǐ.

Yes.

» 3. 请客 Stand treat

A：说好了，今天我请客。
　　shuō hǎo le, jīn tiān wǒ qǐng kè.

It's my treat today.

B：那不行，上次也是你请客。这次我做东吧。
　　nà bù xíng, shàng cì yě shì nǐ qǐng kè. zhè cì wǒ zuò dōng ba.

No. You paid last time. I'll treat you this time.

A：那好吧。下次我们再聚，机会多得很。
　　nà hǎo ba. xià cì wǒ men zài jù, jī huì duō de hěn.

All right, we'll get together again next time. There's plenty of opportunities.

二、饮　食

核心词汇（Key Words）

序号	词语	拼音	翻译
1	服务员	fú wù yuán	waiter
2	买单	mǎi dān	to pay the bill
3	付款	fù kuǎn	payment
4	微信	wēi xìn	WeChat
5	支付宝	zhī fù bǎo	Alipay
6	现金	xiàn jīn	cash
7	扫码	sǎo mǎ	to scan the code
8	做东	zuò dōng	to play the host
9	请客	qǐng kè	to entertain guests

你知道吗？—— 如何用微信支付？（Do you know?—— How to pay with WeChat?）

1. 点击进入微信。
   diǎn jī jìn rù wēi xìn.

Click to enter WeChat.

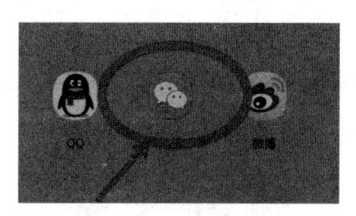

2. 点击右上角的"+"。
   diǎn jī yòu shàng jiǎo de "+".

Click the "+" in the upper right corner.

· 043 ·

留学生实用汉语99例

diǎn jī "sǎo yī sǎo".
3. 点击"扫一扫"。

Click "Scan".

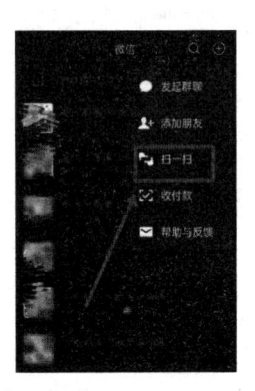

sǎo miáo shāng jiā de èr wéi mǎ.
4. 扫描商家的二维码。

Scan the QR code of the merchant.

shū rù jīn é, diǎn jī "fù kuǎn".
5. 输入金额,点击"付款"。

Enter the amount and click "Pay".

二、饮 食

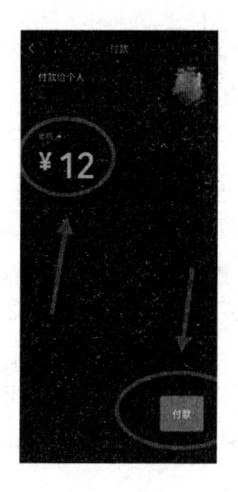

dǎ bāo
打 包
Packing

核心句子 (Kernel Sentence)

bāng wǒ ná yí gè dǎ bāo hé.
1. 帮我拿一个打包盒。

Get me a to-go box.

"打"在这里是动词，意为捆；"包"这里也是动词，意为包装。"打包"的意思是用袋子装好食物。"打包盒"是用于装食物的盒子，一般为一次性的塑料盒，需要额外付费。

"dǎ" is a verb here, meaning bundle; "bāo" is also a verb here, which means packing. "dǎ bāo" means packing food in bags. A "dǎ bāo hé" (packing box)is a box used to hold food, which is usually a disposable plastic box and requires extra payment.

2. 是在这儿吃还是打包带走？
　　shì zài zhèr chī hái shì dǎ bāo dài zǒu?

Is that for here or to go?

"打包带走"的意思是到餐馆点餐后，不在餐馆吃而是带走吃，或是将吃不完的食物用打包盒装好带走。

"dǎ bāo dài zǒu" means that after ordering food in a restaurant, taking it away instead of eating in a restaurant, or packing and taking away the leftover.

3. 这个打包盒不能直接放微波炉。
　　zhè ge dǎ bāo hé bù néng zhí jiē fàng wēi bō lú.

You can't put this to-go box in the microwave oven.

不是所有的打包盒都可以直接放进微波炉加热的。市面上常见的打包盒主要用到 PET、PP、PS 3 种材料，其中只有 PP 材料才能进微波炉。打包盒上有三角箭头标志，其中数字为 5，就是合格材质，是可以放进微波炉加热的。

Not all packing boxes can be heated directly in the microwave oven. The common packing boxes in the market are mainly made of PET, PP and PS, among which only PP can be heated in the microwave oven. There is a triangle arrow mark on the packing box, in which the number is 5, which is a qualified material and can be heated in a microwave oven.

实用场景（The Practical Situation）

» 1. 在饭馆打包食物 Packing food in a restaurant

A：实在吃不完，我们打包带回去吧。
　　shí zài chī bù wán, wǒ men dǎ bāo dài huí qu ba.

We can't finish it. Let's take it home.

B：好的，免得浪费。
　　hǎo de, miǎn de làng fèi.

All right, so we don't waste it.

二、饮　食

A：服务员，帮我拿一个打包盒。

Excuse me, get me a to-go box, please.

B：好的。

OK.

A：谢谢，麻烦帮我把这个打包。

Thanks, please wrap this up for me.

» 2. 在食堂打包食物 Packing food in the cafeteria

A：同学，是在这儿吃还是打包带走？

Student, for here or to go?

B：打包带走。

Take away.

A：好的。

OK.

» 3. 加热打包食物 Heating packaged food

A：这是昨天从饭店打包回来的鸡汤，今天中午把它吃完。

This is the chicken soup I packed from the restaurant yesterday, and we have to finish it today for lunch.

B：等一下。这个打包盒不能直接放微波炉的。要换一个碗。

Wait a minute. You can't put this to-go box in the microwave oven. We need to change it with a bowl.

A：哦，我忘记了，幸亏你提醒了我。

Oh, I forget. It's a good thing you remind me.

B：放在冰箱的熟食品取出后一定回锅再热一热。不然吃了可能会拉肚子呢。

The coOKed food which is taken out from the refrigerator must return to the pot to heat up again. Otherwise, you may have diarrhea after eating it.

A：好的。

OK.

核心词汇（Key Words）

序号	词语	拼音	翻译
1	打包盒	dǎ bāo hé	to-go box
2	打包	dǎ bāo	to pack
3	浪费	làng fèi	to waste
4	带走	dài zǒu	to take away
5	加热	jiā rè	to heat

二、饮 食

> ☞ **你知道吗？**—— **光盘行动**（Do you know?——"Clear your plate" campaign）

节约是中华民族传统美德之一。光盘行动由一群热心公益的人们发起，光盘行动的宗旨：餐厅不多点、食堂不多打、厨房不多做。养成生活中珍惜粮食、反对浪费的习惯。并且提醒与告诫人们：饥饿距离我们并不遥远，我们要珍惜粮食。

——参考360百科"光盘行动"
https://baike.so.com/doc/5351151-5586608.html

Diligent and thrifty is one of the traditional virtues of the Chinese nation. The "clear your plate" campaign was initiated by a group of people who are enthusiastic about public welfare. The tenet of the campaign is that ordering just enough in restaurants, buying just enough in canteens and coOKing just enough in kitchens. The campaign calls for developing the habit of cherishing food and opposing waste in life. It reminds and warns people that hunger is not far away from us, so we should cherish food.

diǎn wài mài
点 外 卖
Ordering takeouts

> ☞ **核心句子**（Kernel Sentence）

yào bù wǒ men diǎn wài mài chī ba ?
1. 要不我们点外卖吃吧？
Why don't we order some take-away food?

"外卖"在这里是名词，指售卖供顾客带离店铺的食品（一般指自己店铺现做的），提供外送服务。

"wài mài" here is a noun that refers to the sale of food(usually freshly made by one's own store) for customers to take away from a store.

2. 您点的外卖到了，请下楼来取一下。
   nín diǎn de wài mài dào le, qǐng xià lóu lái qǔ yí xià.

Your take-away food has arrived. Please come down to get it.

"点"在这里是动词，也可以换成"叫"，"点外卖"也可以说成"叫外卖"。

"diǎn" is a verb here and can also be changed to "jiào", while "diǎn wài mài" can also be said as "jiào wài mài".

3. 我刚刚点了一份炸鸡，请问什么时候可以送到？
   wǒ gāng gāng diǎn le yí fèn zhá jī, qǐng wèn shén me shí hou kě yǐ sòng dào?

I just ordered some fried chicken. When will it be delivered?

"送到"是个动词，意为把某东西送交到某人手里。也可以换成"送达"，但"送到"更为口语化，日常使用更多。

"sòng dào" is a verb meaning to deliver something to someone. It can also be changed to "sòng dá", but "sòng dào" is more colloquial and more commonly used.

实用场景（The Practical Situation）

» 1. 点外卖吃 Ordering takeaway

A：玛丽，你晚上吃什么？外面在下雨。
   mǎ lì, nǐ wǎnshang chī shén me? wài miàn zài xià yǔ.

What are you having for dinner, Mary? It's raining outside.

B：我也不知道，要不我们点外卖吃吧？
wǒ yě bù zhī dào, yào bù wǒ men diǎn wài mài chī ba?

I don't know. Why don't we order takeout?

A：好呀，点什么呢？
hǎo ya, diǎn shén me ne?

OK, what shall I order?

B：点比萨吧。
diǎn bǐ sà ba.

The pizza.

» 2. 外卖食物到了 Takeaway food arrived

A：喂，您点的外卖到了，请下楼来取一下。
wèi, nín diǎn de wài mài dào le, qǐng xià lóu lái qǔ yí xià.

Hello, your takeaway has arrived. Please come down and get it.

B：好的，我马上下来。
hǎo de, wǒ mǎ shàng xià lai.

OK, I'll be right down.

» 3. 外卖什么时候送到？ When will the takeaway be delivered?

A：喂，您好，我刚刚点了一份炸鸡，请问什么时候可以送到？
wèi, nín hǎo, wǒ gāng gāng diǎn le yí fèn zhá jī, qǐng wèn shén me shí hou kě yǐ sòng dào?

Hello, I just ordered some fried chicken. When will it be delivered?

B：您留的地址是阳光小区五栋吗？
nín liú de dì zhǐ shì yáng guāng xiǎo qū wǔ dòng ma?

Is the address you left Building 5, Yang Guang Community?

A：<ruby>是<rt>shì</rt></ruby><ruby>的<rt>de</rt></ruby>。

Yes.

B：<ruby>我<rt>wǒ</rt></ruby><ruby>查<rt>chá</rt></ruby><ruby>一<rt>yí</rt></ruby><ruby>下<rt>xià</rt></ruby>，<ruby>噢<rt>ō</rt></ruby>，<ruby>大概<rt>dà gài</rt></ruby><ruby>在<rt>zài</rt></ruby> 19:24 <ruby>送达<rt>sòng dá</rt></ruby>。

Let me check. Oh, It will arrive around 19:24.

A：<ruby>好的<rt>hǎo de</rt></ruby>，<ruby>谢谢<rt>xiè xie</rt></ruby>！

OK, thanks!

核心词汇（Key Words）

序号	词语	拼音	翻译
1	外卖	wài mài	take-away food
2	比萨	bǐ sà	pizza
3	炸鸡	zhá jī	fried chicken
4	地址	dì zhǐ	address
5	取	qǔ	take

你知道吗？——如何点外卖？（Do you know?—— How to order takeout？）

点外卖是一个非常必要的生存技能，可以不出门就享受到美食，那么我们要经历哪些点餐步骤呢？

Ordering takeout is a very necessary survival skill, you can enjoy the food without going out, so what steps should we go through to order food?

第一步，下载一个"美团"外卖 App。

Step 1, you have to download Meituan delivery App.

二、饮　食

第二步，打开美团 App，在首页选择"外卖"图标。

Step 2, open the Meituan App and select the "Take-out" icon on the home page.

第三步，在"搜索"里输入想吃的食物名称。

Step 3, enter the name of the food you want in search box.

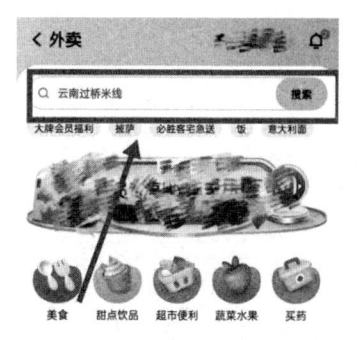

· 053 ·

第四步，选择一家满意的店铺点进去看看。

Step 4, you can choose a satisfactory store and have a look.

第五步，选择好自己想要吃的食物，点击界面上的"+"，表示你购买的数量。

Step 5, choose the food you want to eat, click "+" on the interface, indicating the amount you buy.

二、饮　食

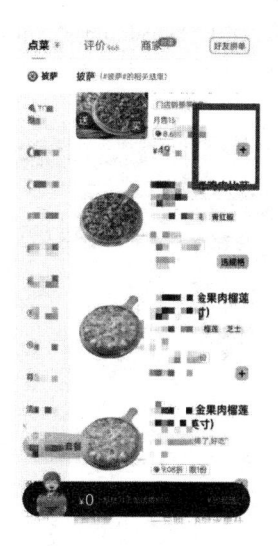

第六步，点击左下角的购物车图标。点击"去结算"。

Step 6, click the shopping cart icon in the lower left corner. Click "Go to Checkout".

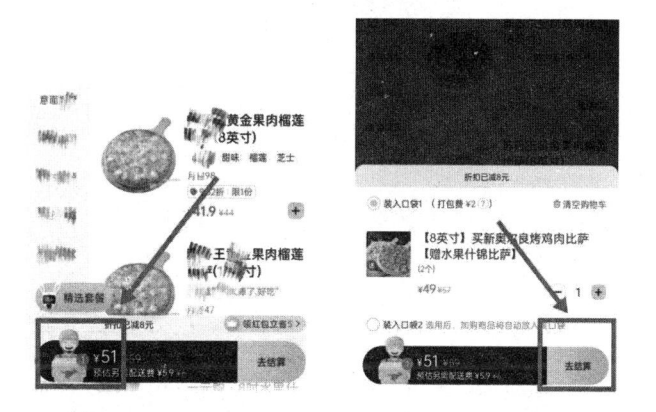

第七步，确认无误后，点击"提交订单"，填写"选择收货地址"，然后付款等候菜品送达即可。

Step 7, once you're sure, click "Submit order", fill in "Select delivery address", then pay and wait for the food to arrive.

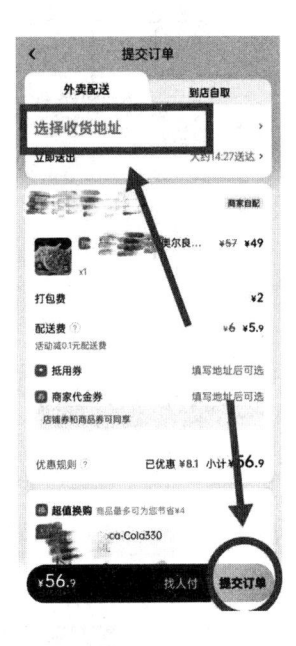

三、购物 (gòu wù)
Shopping

逛菜场 (guàng cài chǎng)
Go to the market

> **核心句子**（Kernel Sentence）

1. 牛肉怎么卖？ (niú ròu zěn me mài?)

How much is the beef?

"怎么"是疑问代词，询问方式。在这里是询问牛肉的价格，还可以这样问："牛肉多少钱一斤？"一般回答是"……元一斤"。

"zěn me" is an interrogative pronoun, it is a way of asking means and ways. In this case, it's used to ask about the price of beef. You can also ask "niú ròu duō shǎo qián yì jīn". The general answer is "…yuán yì jīn."

2. 你想买点儿什么？ (nǐ xiǎng mǎi diǎnr shén me?)

What do you want to buy?

卖东西的人招呼客人时，通常会问"你想买点儿什么"或者"你想要点儿什么"。

When a seller greets a customer, he usually asks, "nǐ xiǎng mǎi diǎnr shén me?" Or "nǐ xiǎng yào diǎnr shén me?"(What do you want to buy?)

· 057 ·

3. kě yǐ pián yi yì diǎnr ma?
可以便宜一点儿吗？

Can you make it a little cheaper?

一般情况下，在商场和超市是明码标价，不能讨价还价的。但是在农贸市场、菜场或者一些小店，还是可以还价的。最终价格能便宜多少，要看买家的还价能力了。

Under normal circumstances, the price is clearly marked in shopping malls and supermarkets, and no bargaining is allowed. But in the farmer's market, food market or some small shops, you can still make a counter-offer. How much cheaper the final price can be depends on the buyer's bargaining power.

实用场景（The Practical Situation）

» 1. 询问价格 Asking the price

A：lǎo bǎn, qǐng wèn niú ròu zěn me mài?
老板，请问牛肉怎么卖？

Excuse me, Sir. How much is the beef?

B：niú ròu 40 yuán yì jīn.
牛肉 40 元一斤。

Beef is 40 *yuan* a catty.

A：zhū ròu duō shǎo qián yì jīn ne?
猪肉多少钱一斤呢？

How much is the pork?

B：zhū ròu 15 yuán yì jīn.
猪肉 15 元一斤。

Pork is 15 *yuan* a catty.

A：好的，我要一斤牛肉和两斤猪肉。

OK. I'd like one catty of beef and two catties of pork.

B：一共70元。

70 *yuan* altogether.

2. 还价 Counter-offer

A：请问苹果多少钱一斤？

How much is the apple?

B：6元一斤。

It's 6 *yuan* a catty.

A：我多买些苹果，价格可以便宜一点儿吗？

I'll buy some more apples. Can you give me a lower price?

B：那就5元一斤。

5 *yuan* a catty, then.

A：好，来4斤。

OK, give me 4 catties, please.

B：好的，一共20元。

OK, 20 *yuan* altogether.

» 3. 对比价格 Comparing prices

A：要买点什么？你看看这萝卜多新鲜，白菜也不错。
　　yào mǎi diǎn shén me? nǐ kàn kan zhè luó bo duō xīn xiān, bái cài yě bú cuò.

What do you want to buy? Look, how fresh the radish is! And the cabbage is good, too.

B：萝卜怎么卖？
　　luó bo zěn me mài?

How much are the radishes?

A：2 块一斤。
　　kuài yì jīn.

2 *yuan* a catty.

B：这么贵！你比别人卖得贵，那边的才卖 1.5 元一斤。
　　zhè me guì! nǐ bǐ bié rén mài de guì, nà biān de cái mài 1.5 yuán yì jīn.

So expensive! You sell more expensively than the others. They sell only 1.5 *yuan* a catty over there.

A：你看看我的萝卜比别人卖的萝卜新鲜多了。
　　nǐ kàn kan wǒ de luó bo bǐ bié rén mài de luó bo xīn xiān duō le.

Look at my radishes. They are much fresher than others.

B：行吧，那就买两斤吧。
　　xíng ba, nà jiù mǎi liǎng jīn ba.

OK, then I'll buy two catties.

☞ 核心词汇 (Key Words)

序号	词语	拼音	翻译
1	牛肉	niú ròu	beef
2	猪肉	zhū ròu	pork
3	鸡肉	jī ròu	chicken

三、购 物

续 表

序 号	词 语	拼 音	翻 译
4	羊肉	yáng ròu	mutton
5	斤	jīn	catty/jin(a unit of weight =0.5 kilograms)
6	元	yuán	*yuan*
7	一共	yí gòng	a total of
8	苹果	píng guǒ	apple
9	梨子	lí zi	pear
10	萝卜	luó bo	radish
11	白菜	bái cài	Chinese cabbage
12	新鲜	xīn xiān	fresh
13	便宜	pián yi	cheap

☞ 你知道吗？——"斤"【Do you know?——"jin"（catty）】

在菜市场，人们一般使用的重量基本单位是"斤"，等于0.5公斤或1.102磅。

In China, the basic unit of weight used in food markets is "jin" (catty), which is equal to 0.5 kilograms or 1.102 pounds.

逛 超 市
guàng chāo shì

Go to the supermarket

☞ 核心句子（Kernel Sentence）

1. 您好，这里有购物车和购物篮，您可以自取。
   nín hǎo, zhè lǐ yǒu gòu wù chē hé gòu wù lán, nín kě yǐ zì qǔ.

Hello, here are shopping carts and baskets. You can pick them up by yourself.

· 061 ·

一般超市的购物车和购物篮都放置在超市门口，顾客可以根据自己的购物量选择。有的购物车需要投币才能解锁使用，有的是直接可以使用的。无论是购物车还是购物篮一般都不允许拿出超市，最多使用到停车场门口。

Generally, shopping carts and shopping baskets in supermarkets are placed at the entrance of supermarkets, and customers can choose according to their own shopping volume. Some shopping carts need coins to unlock, while others can be used directly. Shopping carts and shopping baskets are generally not allowed to be taken out of the supermarket, but they are permitted to use at the parking lot door utmost.

2. 在哪儿称重？
   zài nǎr chēngzhòng?

Where can I weigh it?

超市里有些销售的食品没有进行包装，也就是散装食品。散装食品因为节省了烦琐的包装，降低了食品的价格，很受消费者欢迎。在选好食品的数量后，需要到附近的称重处称重、计算价格。

Some foods sold in supermarkets are unpackaged, these are bulk foods. Bulk foods are very popular with consumers because they save complicated packaging and reduce the price of food. After selecting the quantity of food, you need to weigh and calculate the price at the nearby weighing place.

3. 一共消费87元，请问您有会员卡吗？
   yí gòngxiāo fèi 87 yuán, qǐngwèn nín yǒu huì yuán kǎ ma?

The total cost is 87 *yuan*. Do you have a membership card?

很多超市实行会员制，如会员积分、会员商品打折等。微信、支付宝、现金、刷卡等支付方式都接受。

Many supermarkets implement the membership system, such as membership points, discounts and so on. WeChat, Alipay, cash, credit card and other payment methods are accepted.

三、购　物

实用场景（The Practical Situation）

» 1. 超市优惠活动 Supermarket promotions

A：您好，这里有购物车和购物篮，您可以自取。

Hello, here are shopping carts and baskets. You can pick them up by yourself.

B：好的，谢谢。

OK, thanks.

A：这是本月的优惠广告，你可以看看，有很多商品在打折。

This is the discount advertisement for this month. You can have a look. There are many products on sale.

B：好的。谢谢！优惠活动什么时候开始？

All right. Thank you. When does the special offer start?

A：今天开始后天结束。

It starts today and ends the day after tomorrow.

B：好的，那今天多买一些。

OK. Buy more stuff today.

» 2. 购买散装食品 Buying bulk food

A：不好意思，这些散装零食需要称重。

Sorry, these bulk snacks need to be weighed.

· 063 ·

B：在哪儿称重？

Where can I weigh it?

A：可以找你选购零食区的售货员。称完之后会有条形码。

You can find the clerk in the snack section. There will be a bar code after the weighing.

B：好的，谢谢。

OK, thanks.

A：不客气。

You're welcome.

3. 办理会员卡 Applying for membership card

A：您好，一共消费87元，请问有会员卡吗？

Hello, the total cost is 87 *yuan*. Do you have a membership card?

B：没有。

No.

A：会员可以打九折，需要办理吗？

There is a 10% discount for members. Do you need to apply for it?

B：不用了，谢谢。

No, thanks.

三、购　物

☞ 核心词汇（Key Words）

序号	词语	拼音	翻译
1	购物车	gòu wù chē	shopping cart
2	购物篮	gòu wù lán	shopping basket
3	优惠广告	yōu huì guǎng gào	preferential AD
4	商品	shāng pǐn	goods
5	打折	dǎ zhé	at a discount
6	零食	líng shí	snacks
7	称重	chēng zhòng	to weigh
8	条形码	tiáo xíng mǎ	bar code
9	会员卡	huì yuán kǎ	membership card
10	售货员	shòu huò yuán	salesman

☞ 你知道吗？—— 中国的超市文化（Do you know?—— Supermarket culture in China）

在有超市之前，中国人多数在一些杂货店购买日常生活的货品。在20世纪90年代初期，超市文化渐渐进入中国。超市受欢迎的原因是商品种类很多，没有假货，而且购物环境舒适，每个超市基本都有购物车和购物篮供顾客选用。超市已经成为很多人购物的首选场所了。

Before supermarkets appeared in China, most Chinese people bought their daily goods at some grocery store. In the early 1990s, supermarket culture gradually entered China. The reason why supermarkets are popular is that there are many kinds of goods, no fake goods, and the shopping environment is comfortable. Every supermarket basically has shopping carts and baskets for customers to use. Supermarkets have become the first choice for many people.

guàng shāng chǎng
逛 商 场
Go to the mall

☞ 核心句子（Kernel Sentence）

xiǎng qù nǎr guàng?
1. 想去哪儿逛？

Where do you want to go?

"逛"是动词，意为四处走一走，看一看，如"逛超市""逛菜市场""逛夜市""逛街"。

"guàng" is a verb that means to walk around and have a look, like "guàng chāo shì"(to go to a supermarket), "guàng cài shì chǎng"(to go to a vegetable market), "guàng yè shì"(to go to a night market),"guàng jiē"(to go shopping).

zhè tiáo lián yī qún kàn qǐ lai bú cuò, wǒ néng shì shi ma?
2. 这条连衣裙看起来不错，我能试试吗？

This dress looks nice. Can I try it on?

这里的"看"的意思是经过观察，从表面判断、估计某种情况，这里也可以用"看上去"。

"kàn" here means to judge or estimate a situation from the surface by observing it. We can also use "kàn shàng qu" here.

yuán jià 400 yuán, xiàn zài dǎ bā zhé, 320 yuán.
3. 原价400元，现在打八折，320元。

The original price is 400 *yuan*, and now it's 20 percent off, 320 *yuan*.

"打折"意思是降低商品的定价出售，如"打八折"就是原价的80%。

"dǎ zhé" means to sell an item at a lower price, for example, "dǎ bā zhé" is 80% of the original price.

三、购 物

🖝 实用场景（The Practical Situation）

» 1. 去逛商场 Go shopping

A：我想买条裤子，今天星期天，我们去逛商场吧。

I want to buy a pair of pants. It's Sunday. Let's go shopping.

B：想去哪儿逛？

Where do you want to go?

A：去万达吧，那里特别大，1楼到2楼是卖衣服的，4楼是吃饭的地方，正好中午我们可以在那儿吃饭。

Go to Wanda. It is very big. From the first floor to the third floor there are many clothes shops, and the fourth floor is a place to eat. We can have lunch there at noon.

B：好啊。

Good.

» 2. 试穿衣服 Trying on clothes

A：欢迎光临，喜欢的都可以试穿。

Welcome. You can try on anything you like.

B：这条连衣裙看起来不错，我能试试吗？

This dress looks nice. Can I try it on?

A：dāng rán kě yǐ．nǐ chuān duō shǎo mǎ de？
当然可以。你穿多少码的？

Sure. What size do you wear?

B：M mǎ．
M 码。

Middle size.

A：hǎo de，shì yī jiān zài nà biān．
好的，试衣间在那边。

OK, the fitting room is over there.

3. 换大一码 Changing one size

A：zěn me yàng？
怎么样？

How about the clothes?

B：yǒu diǎnr jǐn．
有点儿紧。

It's a little tight.

A：nà ná dà yí hào de nín shì shi ba．
那拿大一号的您试试吧。

Then try the larger size.

B：hǎo de．
好的。

Okay.

A：zhè jiàn zěn me yàng？
这件怎么样？

How about this one?

三、购 物

B：这件挺合适的。多少钱？
zhè jiàn tǐng hé shì de. duō shǎo qián?

It fits me perfectly. How much is it?

A：原价400元，现在打八折，320元。
yuán jià 400 yuán, xiàn zài dǎ bā zhé, 320 yuán.

The original price is 400 *yuan*, and now it's 20 percent off, 320 *yuan*.

核心词汇（Key Words）

序号	词语	拼音	翻译
1	逛街	guàng jiē	to go shopping
2	裤子	kù zi	trousers
3	裙子	qún zi	skirt
4	衬衣	chèn yī	shirt
5	商场	shāng chǎng	mall
6	试穿	shì chuān	to try it on
7	看起来	kàn qǐ lai	to look
8	试衣间	shì yī jiān	fitting room
9	合适	hé shì	appropriate
10	原价	yuán jià	original price

你知道吗？—— 换季促销（Do you know?—— BIG OFF）

商场一般会在换季的时候打折促销，如一月和七月。还有店庆、国庆节、劳动节等节假日的时候也会清仓打折。打折就是在原来售价的基础上降价销售，几折则表示实际售价占原来售价的成数。打八折就原价的80%，打两折就是原价的20%。

计算方法为：原价×（1-折扣）。

原价是100元，打一折，就是：100×0.1=10。

Shopping malls usually offer discounts at the end of the seasons, such as January and July. On store celebrations, National Day, Labor Day and other holidays there will also be clearance discounts. A discount is a sale on the basis of the original selling price. For example, a 20% discount is 80% of the original price. An 80% discount is 20% of the original price.

The calculation method is: original price ×(1-discount).

The original price is 100 *yuan*, 90% discount, is : 100×0.1=10.

网上购物
Shopping online

核心句子 (Kernel Sentence)

1. 在网上买东西既方便又便宜。

It's convenient and cheap to buy things online.

"既 A 又 B" 表示两种情况都有,如 "既聪明又努力"。

"jì A yòu B" means both, such as "both smart and hard working".

现在中国网上购物非常流行,网购给人们的生活带来了很多方便。在网购平台不仅可以买到中国货,外国货也可以很容易地买到,如咖啡、衣服、奶粉、护肤品等。但一定要在正规的平台进行交易,比较受欢迎的网站有"淘宝网""京东""当当""拼多多"等。

Online shopping is very popular in China now. Online shopping brings a lot of convenience to people's life. Not only can Chinese goods be bought on online shopping platforms, but also foreign goods can be easily bought, such as coffee, clothes, milk powder, skin care products and so on. But it must be done on formal platforms. Taobao, JD.com, Dangdang and Pinduoduo are all popular shopping websites.

2. 请问这件连衣裙有货吗？
   qǐngwèn zhè jiàn lián yī qún yǒu huò ma?

Is this dress in stock?

有的时候你想要买的东西可能卖完了，那么即使你付款了商家也不会发货，所以可以问一问商家的客服是否有货。

Sometimes the item you want to buy may be sold out, and the merchant will not deliver it even if you pay for it, so you can ask the merchant's customer service staff if it is available.

3. 亲，喜欢可以下单试试呢。
   qīn, xǐ huan kě yǐ xià dān shì shi ne.

Dear, if you like, you can have a try.

"亲"在这里是"亲爱的"的缩略形式，意为"亲爱的顾客"。

"Qīn" here is a shortened form of "qīn ài de"(dear), which means "qīn ài de gù kè"(dear customer).

实用场景（The Practical Situation）

» 1. 网上买东西 Buy things online

A：麦克，你的衣服真好看，是在哪儿买的？
   mài kè, nǐ de yī fu zhēn hǎo kàn, shì zài nǎr mǎi de?

Mike, your dress looks nice. Where did you buy it?

B：网上买的。
   wǎngshàng mǎi de.

Online.

· 071 ·

A：nǐ jīng cháng zài wǎng shàng mǎi dōng xi ma?
你经常在网上买东西吗?

Do you often buy things online?

B：shì ya, zài wǎng shàng mǎi dōng xi jì fāng biàn yòu pián yi.
是呀,在网上买东西既方便又便宜。

Yeah, it's convenient and cheap to buy things online.

» 2. 向客服咨询 Consulting the customer service

A：qǐng wèn zhè jiàn lián yī qún yǒu huò ma?
请问这件连衣裙有货吗?

Is this dress in stock?

B：qīn, yǒu de. nín shēn gāo、tǐ zhòng duō shǎo?
亲,有的。您身高、体重多少?

Honey, yes. What's your height and weight?

A：wǒ 160 lí mǐ, 98 jīn, chuān shén me mǎ hé shì?
我160厘米,98斤,穿什么码合适?

I am 160 centimeters,98 catties, what size to wear appropriate?

B：S mǎ huì bǐ jiào hé shì.
S码会比较合适。

S code would be more appropriate.

» 3. 询问发货时间 Asking about delivery time

A：qīn, xǐ huan kě yǐ xià dān shì shi ne, shōu dào huò bú huì ràng qīn shī wàng de.
亲,喜欢可以下单试试呢,收到货不会让亲失望的。

Honey,if you like, you can place an order and try it. You won't be disappointed when you receive the goods.

三、购　物

B：<ruby>好<rt>hǎo</rt></ruby><ruby>的<rt>de</rt></ruby>。<ruby>请<rt>qǐng</rt></ruby><ruby>问<rt>wèn</rt></ruby><ruby>什<rt>shén</rt></ruby><ruby>么<rt>me</rt></ruby><ruby>时<rt>shí</rt></ruby><ruby>候<rt>hou</rt></ruby><ruby>发<rt>fā</rt></ruby><ruby>货<rt>huò</rt></ruby>？

OK. When will the goods be delivered?

A：3—5 <ruby>天<rt>tiān</rt></ruby>哦。

3 to 5 days.

B：<ruby>那<rt>nà</rt></ruby><ruby>什<rt>shén</rt></ruby><ruby>么<rt>me</rt></ruby><ruby>时<rt>shí</rt></ruby><ruby>候<rt>hou</rt></ruby><ruby>可<rt>kě</rt></ruby><ruby>以<rt>yǐ</rt></ruby><ruby>收<rt>shōu</rt></ruby><ruby>到<rt>dào</rt></ruby><ruby>货<rt>huò</rt></ruby>？

When can I receive the goods?

A：<ruby>一<rt>yì</rt></ruby><ruby>般<rt>bān</rt></ruby><ruby>发<rt>fā</rt></ruby><ruby>货<rt>huò</rt></ruby><ruby>后<rt>hòu</rt></ruby><ruby>三<rt>sān</rt></ruby><ruby>天<rt>tiān</rt></ruby><ruby>左<rt>zuǒ</rt></ruby><ruby>右<rt>yòu</rt></ruby>。<ruby>你<rt>nǐ</rt></ruby><ruby>可<rt>kě</rt></ruby><ruby>以<rt>yǐ</rt></ruby><ruby>查<rt>chá</rt></ruby><ruby>看<rt>kàn</rt></ruby><ruby>物<rt>wù</rt></ruby><ruby>流<rt>liú</rt></ruby><ruby>信<rt>xìn</rt></ruby><ruby>息<rt>xī</rt></ruby>。

Generally about three days after delivery. You can check the logistics information.

核心词汇（Key Words）

序号	词语	拼音	翻译
1	上网	shàng wǎng	surf the Internet
2	网上购物	wǎng shàng gòu wù	online shopping
3	方便	fāng biàn	convenient
4	收货	shōu huò	to receive goods
5	发货	fā huò	to deliver goods
6	物流信息	wù liú xìn xī	the logistics information
7	客服	kè fú	customer service
8	亲	qīn	honey

你知道吗？——如何在网上购物？（Do you know?—— How to shop online？）

第一步，打开淘宝 App，点击"搜索"，查找自己想买的商品。

Step 1: Open the Taobao App and click "search" to find the goods you want to buy.

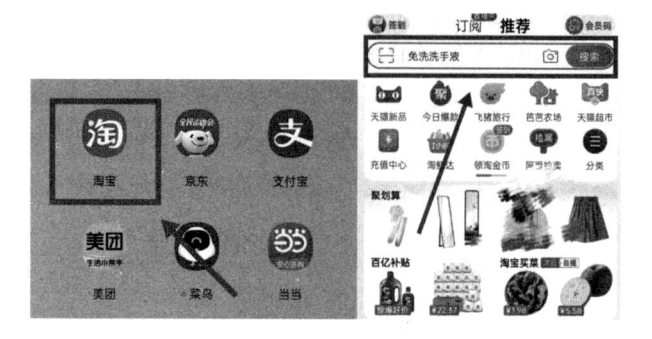

第二步，选定好要买的，点击下方"加入购物车"或者"马上抢"。

Step 2: Select what you want and click "Add to cart" or "Grab it now".

三、购物

第三步，选定喜欢的商品，然后提交订单付款。

Step 3: Choose what you like, then submit the order for payment.

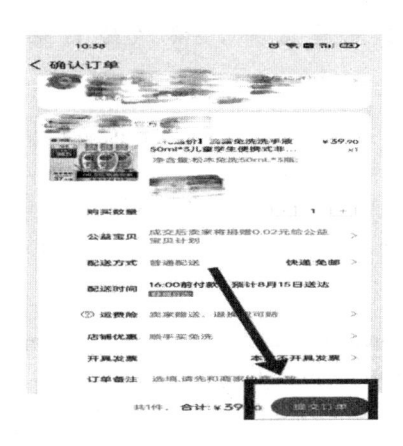

注：这里我们只介绍如何使用淘宝 App 网上购物，不涉及其他。

wǎng shàng tuì huàn huò
网上退换货
Online return and exchange

☞ 核心句子（Kernel Sentence）

nín shì xiǎng tuì hái shi xiǎng huàn ne ?
1. 您 是 想 退 还 是 想 换 呢？

Do you want to return it or exchange it?

这里的"退"，指的是"退货"；"换"的意思是"换货"。因为在网上购物无法触摸到真实的货物，所以有时候会买到不合适的货物。这个时候就需要买家和商家商量是退货还是换货。

The "tuì" here refers to "return"; "huàn" means "exchange". Because you can't touch real goods when shopping online, sometimes you may get the inappropriate goods. At this time, buyers and merchants need to discuss whether to return or exchange goods.

2. 好的，您申请退款，按照给的地址寄回来就行了。邮费自付哦。

OK, you apply for a refund and send it back to the address given. Postage pays.

如果您申请退货后，商家同意退货，那么系统会自动发给您退货地址，您只需要去快递站寄出快递就可以了。最后，一定不要忘记在系统里上传寄快递的物流单号。

If the merchant agrees to return the goods after your applying , the system will automatically send you the return address. You just need to go to the express station to send the goods. Finally, don't forget to upload and send the express logistics number in the system.

3. 我买的连衣裙码数发错了。

The dress I bought was given the wrong size.

中国常见服装有两种型号标法：一是 S（小）、M（中）、L（大）、XL（加大）；二是身高加胸围的形式，如 160/80A、165/85A、170/85A 等。在中国的服装型号标准 GB/T 1335 中，女装上衣 S 号（小号）的号型是 155/80A；M 号（中号）为 160/84A；L 号（大号）为 165/88A。"号"是指服装的长短，"型"是指服装的肥瘦。例如 165/88A，斜线前后的数字表示人体高度和人的胸围或腰围，斜线后面的字母表示人的体型特征。Y 型指胸大腰细的体型，A 型表示一般体型，B 型表示微胖体型，C 型表示胖体型，区别体型的方法是看胸围减去腰围的数值。

——参考 360 百科"尺码"https://baike.so.com/doc/572663-24907753.html

There are two types of common clothing in China: one is S (small), M (medium), L (large) and XL (extra large); Second, height plus chest circumference, such as 160/80A, 165/85A, 170/85A, etc. In China's clothing model standard GB/T 1335, the size of women's tops S (small) is 155/80 A; M (medium) is 160/84A; L (large) is 165/88A.

"Size" refers to the length of clothing, and "type" refers to the thinness of clothing. For example, 165/88A, the numbers before and after the diagonal line indicate the height of human body and the bust or waist circumference of human body, and the letters behind the diagonal line indicate the body shape characteristics of human body. Y-type refers to the body shape with big chest and thin waist, A-type represents general body shape, B-type represents slightly fat body shape, and C-type represents fat body shape. The method to distinguish body shape is to look at the value of chest circumference minus waist circumference.

实用场景 (The Practical Situation)

» 1. 换货 Exchanging goods

A: 你好，我买的连衣裙有点儿小，订单号是 4327589083736。
　　nǐ hǎo, wǒ mǎi de lián yī qún yǒu diǎnr xiǎo, dìng dān hào shì 4327589083736.

Hello, the dress I bought is a little small. The order number is 4327589083736.

B: 好的，您是想退还是想换呢？
　　hǎo de, nín shì xiǎng tuì hái shi xiǎng huàn ne?

OK, do you want to return it or exchange it?

A: 能给我换件大一号的吗？
　　néng gěi wǒ huàn jiàn dà yí hào de ma?

Can you exchange it for a larger size?

B: 好的。
　　hǎo de.

Alright.

» 2. 退货 Returning the goods

A: 你好，我要退货。
　　nǐ hǎo, wǒ yào tuì huò.

Hi, I'd like to return this.

· 077 ·

B：<ruby>亲<rt>qīn</rt></ruby> <ruby>对<rt>duì</rt></ruby> <ruby>我们<rt>wǒ men</rt></ruby> <ruby>的<rt>de</rt></ruby> <ruby>连衣裙<rt>lián yī qún</rt></ruby> <ruby>有<rt>yǒu</rt></ruby> <ruby>什么<rt>shén me</rt></ruby> <ruby>不满意<rt>bù mǎn yì</rt></ruby> <ruby>的<rt>de</rt></ruby> <ruby>吗<rt>ma</rt></ruby>？

What's wrong with our dresses?

A：<ruby>连衣裙<rt>lián yī qún</rt></ruby> <ruby>质量<rt>zhì liàng</rt></ruby> <ruby>没有<rt>méi yǒu</rt></ruby> <ruby>问题<rt>wèn tí</rt></ruby>，<ruby>是<rt>shì</rt></ruby> <ruby>我<rt>wǒ</rt></ruby> <ruby>自己<rt>zì jǐ</rt></ruby> <ruby>不<rt>bú</rt></ruby> <ruby>适合<rt>shì hé</rt></ruby>。

There is nothing wrong with the quality of the dress, but it doesn't fit me.

B：<ruby>好的<rt>hǎo de</rt></ruby>，<ruby>麻烦<rt>má fan</rt></ruby> <ruby>你<rt>nǐ</rt></ruby> <ruby>按照<rt>àn zhào</rt></ruby> <ruby>给<rt>gěi</rt></ruby> <ruby>的<rt>de</rt></ruby> <ruby>地址<rt>dì zhǐ</rt></ruby> <ruby>寄<rt>jì</rt></ruby> <ruby>回来<rt>huí lai</rt></ruby>，<ruby>邮费<rt>yóu fèi</rt></ruby> <ruby>自付<rt>zì fù</rt></ruby> <ruby>哦<rt>o</rt></ruby>。

OK, please send it back to the address we gave you and pay the postage yourself.

3. 发错货了 Senting the wrong goods

A：<ruby>你好<rt>nǐ hǎo</rt></ruby>，<ruby>我<rt>wǒ</rt></ruby> <ruby>买<rt>mǎi</rt></ruby> <ruby>的<rt>de</rt></ruby> <ruby>连衣裙<rt>lián yī qún</rt></ruby> <ruby>码数<rt>mǎ shù</rt></ruby> <ruby>发错<rt>fā cuò</rt></ruby> <ruby>了<rt>le</rt></ruby>，<ruby>订单号<rt>dìng dān hào</rt></ruby> <ruby>是<rt>shì</rt></ruby> <ruby>4327589083736<rt>4327589083736</rt></ruby>，<ruby>我<rt>wǒ</rt></ruby> <ruby>买<rt>mǎi</rt></ruby> <ruby>的<rt>de</rt></ruby> <ruby>是<rt>shì</rt></ruby> S <ruby>码<rt>mǎ</rt></ruby>，<ruby>发<rt>fā</rt></ruby> <ruby>给<rt>gěi</rt></ruby> <ruby>我<rt>wǒ</rt></ruby> <ruby>的<rt>de</rt></ruby> <ruby>是<rt>shì</rt></ruby> L <ruby>码的<rt>mǎ de</rt></ruby>。

Hello, The dress I bought was given the wrong size. The order number is 4327589083736. I bought the size S, but the one sent to me was the size L.

B：<ruby>能<rt>néng</rt></ruby> <ruby>拍<rt>pāi</rt></ruby> <ruby>照片<rt>zhào piàn</rt></ruby> <ruby>给<rt>gěi</rt></ruby> <ruby>我<rt>wǒ</rt></ruby> <ruby>看看<rt>kàn kan</rt></ruby> <ruby>吗<rt>ma</rt></ruby>？

Can you take a picture and show me?

A：<ruby>好的<rt>hǎo de</rt></ruby>。

Alright.

核心词汇（Key Words）

序号	词语	拼音	翻译
1	订单号	dìng dān hào	order number

三、购　物

续表

序号	词语	拼音	翻译
2	退货	tuì huò	to return goods
3	换货	huàn huò	to exchange goods
4	型号	xíng hào	model
5	质量	zhì liàng	quality
6	邮费	yóu fèi	postage
7	地址	dì zhǐ	address
8	自付	zì fù	self-pay
9	包邮	bāo yóu	exemption from postage

☞ **你知道吗？——淘宝商城的退货要求**（Do you know?——Return requirements on Taobao Mall）

　　淘宝商城"七天无理由退换货"是指由淘宝商城的卖家向买家提供的一种售后服务。具体为买家从签收商品之时起7天内，未使用商品、未破坏原包装并不影响商家二次销售的情况下，商家应无条件配合买家退换货的申请。

　　一般情况下，非卖家责任，退换货邮费均由买家承担；由于商品存在瑕疵引起的退换货行为所产生的邮费由卖家承担。

Taobao Mall "seven days without reason to return and exchange" refers to a kind of after-sales service provided by Taobao Mall sellers to buyers. Specific for the buyer from the receipt of goods logistics within 7 days, does not use the goods, does not destroy the original packaging and does not affect the sale of merchants, merchants should unconditionally cooperate with the buyer's application for return and exchange.

Under normal circumstances, non-seller responsibility for return and replacement postage are borne by the buyer; Due to the existence of defects in the goods caused by the return behavior generated by the seller to bear the postage.

寄快递
Express delivery

> **核心句子**（Kernel Sentence）

1. 我要寄一个快递。

I want to send an express.

2. 请您先扫一下这里的二维码。填写收货人的地址和电话，还有寄货人的电话。

Please scan the QR code here first. Fill in the address and telephone number of the consignee, and the phone number of the shipper.

以前寄快递都是手写填单子，现在寄快递都是"扫码寄件"，用手机在线填写寄件信息，既方便又高效。

In the past, express delivery was filled out by handwriting, but now it is "scan code delivery". It is convenient and efficient to fill in the sending information online by mobile phone.

3. 请问您需要办理加急业务吗？

Do you need any urgent service?

有时候邮寄急需用品，就希望能够快速到达。这时候可以进行加急，在邮寄包裹的时候向快递员提出加急的要求，办理加急业务即可。

Sometimes urgently needed supplies are mailed in the hope that they can arrive quickly. At this time, you can make an urgent request to the courier when mailing the parcel, and handle the urgent business.

三、购 物

> **实用场景**（The Practical Situation）

» 1. 寄快递 Sending Express

A：你好！我要寄一个快递。
nǐ hǎo! wǒ yào jì yī gè kuài dì.

Hello! I want to send an express.

B：请问您是退货还是寄货？
qǐng wèn nín shì tuì huò hái shì jì huò?

Would you like to return or send?

A：我想给我的朋友寄一个礼物。
wǒ xiǎng gěi wǒ de péng you jì yí gè lǐ wù.

I'd like to send a gift to my friend.

B：好的，请您先扫一下这里的二维码。
hǎo de, qǐng nín xiān sǎo yí xià zhè lǐ de èr wéi mǎ.

OK, please scan the QR code here first.

» 2. 填写快递单 Filling out the courier form

A：请问这个怎么填写？
qǐng wèn zhè ge zěn me tián xiě?

How do I fill this out?

B：这里填写收货人的地址和电话，那里填写寄货人的电话。
zhè lǐ tián xiě shōu huò rén de dì zhǐ hé diàn huà, nà lǐ tián xiě jì huò rén de diàn huà.

Fill in the consignee's address and telephone number here, and the shipper's telephone number there.

A：好的。
hǎo de.

Okay.

· 081 ·

» 3. 快递加急业务 Urgent service

A：请问您需要办理加急业务吗？省内一天就到了，省外第二天就能到。

Do you need any urgent service? It will arrive in one day in the province and the next day outside the province.

B：不需要，谢谢！

No, thanks.

核心词汇（Key Words）

序号	词语	拼音	翻译
1	快递	kuài dì	express delivery
2	寄	jì	send
3	收件人	shōu jiàn rén	recipient
4	寄件人	jì jiàn rén	sender
5	加急	jiā jí	urgent
6	快递站	kuài dì zhàn	express station
7	快递费	kuài dì fèi	express fee
8	取件码	qǔ jiàn mǎ	pick-up code
9	快递单号	kuài dì dān hào	courier number
10	快递员	kuài dì yuán	courier

你知道吗？—— 怎样寄快递？（Do you know?——How to send express?）

第一步，把需要寄出去的东西用袋子或者纸箱装好。

Step one, pack the things you need to mail in bags or cartons.

第二步，选择快递公司。比较常见的有顺丰快递、中通快递、EMS、圆通快递、韵达快递等。

Step two, choose a delivery company. The most common ones are SF Express, ZTO express, EMS, YTO express, Yunda Express and so on.

第三步，将包裹带到快递公司。询问快递工作人员，仔细填写好寄件人和收件人的相关信息。

Step three, take the package to the express company. Ask the courier and fill out the information about the sender and the recipient carefully.

第四步，工作人员会对寄件物品进行称重，根据重量按计费标准收费。

Step four, the staff will weigh the items and charge according to the weight.

第五步，寄件完成。快递底单上面有物流单号，可以通过单号对寄件物品进行物流跟踪。

Step five, mailing completed. There is a logistics tracking number on the express receipt, which can be used to track the logistics of the mailed items.

四、出行
Traveling

坐公交车
Taking a bus

> 核心句子（Kernel Sentence）

1. 我去万达应该坐几路公交车？

Which bus should I take to go to Wanda?

这里的"路"不是道路的意思，是路线的意思。如果想要表达公交车的线路，可用这样的格式"数字 + 路 + 公交车"，如6路公交车。

The word "lù" here does not mean road, it means route. If you want to express the route of the bus, you can use the format "number + lù + gōng jiāo chē", such as "liù lù gōng jiāo chē" (No.6 bus).

2. 6路车从学校到万达要坐几站？

How many stops does the No.6 bus take from school to Wanda?

"从A到B"里A和B都为方位地点，意思是A为起点，B为终点的线路。

In the format "cóng A dào B", both A and B are azimuth points, meaning that A is the starting point and B is the ending point.

3. nǐ kě yǐ zhǎo qí tā chéng kè huàn qián, wǒ men bù zhǎo líng.
你可以找其他乘客换钱，我们不找零。

You can change money with other passengers. We don't give change.

一般来说，公交车司机只能提示乘客上车刷卡、投币，不允许直接接触钱币。如果乘客没有带零钱，司机可以帮助动员其他乘客换零，但自己不能参与换钱。

Generally speaking, bus drivers can only prompt passengers to get on the bus to swipe their cards and insert coins, and are not allowed to directly contact coins. If passengers don't have change, drivers can help mobilize other passengers to change, but they can't participate in changing money.

实用场景（The Practical Situation）

» 1. 坐几路公交车？Which bus should I take？

A：qǐng wèn, wǒ qù wàn dá yīng gāi zuò jǐ lù gōng jiāo chē?
请问，我去万达应该坐几路公交车？

Excuse me, which bus should I take to go to Wanda?

B：nǐ kě yǐ zài gōng jiāo chē zhàn zuò 6 lù gōng jiāo chē, zài wàn dá zhàn xià chē jiù kě yǐ le.
你可以在公交车站坐6路公交车，在万达站下车就可以了。

You can take the No.6 bus at the bus stop and get off at Wanda station.

A：6 lù chē gōng jiāo chē zhàn zài nǎr?
6路车公交车站在哪儿？

Where is the No. 6 bus stop?

B：jiù zài mǎ lù duì miàn, kàn jiàn le ma?
就在马路对面，看见了吗？

It's across the street. Can you see it?

· 085 ·

» 2. 询问公交站 Asking the bus station

A：请问，6路车从学校到万达要坐几站？
qǐng wèn, 6 lù chē cóng xué xiào dào wàn dá yào zuò jǐ zhàn?

Excuse me, how many stops does the No.6 bus take from school to Wanda?

B：这儿有公共汽车时刻表，你可以看看。
zhèr yǒu gōng gòng qì chē shí kè biǎo, nǐ kě yǐ kàn kan.

Here is the bus schedule. You may look at it.

A：好的，我找到了，谢谢！
hǎo de, wǒ zhǎo dào le, xiè xie!

OK, I found it. Thank you!

» 3. 支付公交车票 Paying for bus tickets

A：你好，请刷卡或者投币。
nǐ hǎo, qǐng shuā kǎ huò zhě tóu bì.

Hello, please swipe your card or insert a coin.

B：我没有零钱，怎么办？
wǒ méi yǒu líng qián, zěn me bàn?

I have no change. What shall I do?

A：你可以找其他乘客换一下零钱，我们不找零。如果你经常坐公交车，可以去办理一张电子公交卡，比较方便。
nǐ kě yǐ zhǎo qí tā chéng kè huàn yí xià líng qián, wǒ men bù zhǎo líng. rú guǒ nǐ jīng cháng zuò gōng jiāo chē, kě yǐ qù bàn lǐ yì zhāng diàn zǐ gōng jiāo kǎ, bǐ jiào fāng biàn.

You can change money with other passengers. We don't give change. If you often take the bus, you can go for an electronic bus card, it will be more convenient.

四、出　行

☞ 核心词汇（Key Words）

序号	词语	拼音	翻译
1	公交车	gōng jiāo chē	bus
2	公交站	gōng jiāo zhàn	bus station
3	站	zhàn	station
4	时刻表	shí kè biǎo	timetable
5	公交卡	gōng jiāo kǎ	bus card
6	投币	tóu bì	to coin
7	零钱	líng qián	change
8	乘客	chéng kè	passengers

☞ 你知道吗？——中国的公交车（Do you know? —— Buses in China）

不同城市公交车有不同的种类，票价也不一样，目前公交收费的标准主要有两种：

（1）按人次，即不管乘多少站，换多少次车，只要出站就算一次，每次全程的车站，不管从哪个站到那个站都是几元/人。

（2）按距离，即，乘车距离越远，收费越高，即分段式收费，比如1公里1元。1-2公里2元。

以北京为例，常规公交车10公里（含）内2元，10公里以上部分，每增加1元可乘坐5公里。使用市政交通一卡通刷卡乘坐城市公共电汽车，市域内路段给予普通卡5折，学生卡2.5折优惠；市域外路段享受8折优惠。

——360百科"北京公交"

网址：https://baike.so.com/doc/5386918-5623412.html

There are different types of buses in different cities, and their fares are different. At present, there are two main bus charging standards:

1) Per person, that is, no matter how many stations you take or how many times you change buses, it counts once as long as you leave the station. Every time the entire station, no matter from which station to that station, the fee is a few *yuan*/person.

2) According to the distance, the farther the distance traveled, the higher the charge, that is, the segmented charge, such as 1 *yuan* per kilometer. 2 *yuan* for 1-2 kilometers.

Take Beijing as an example. Conventional buses cost 2 *yuan* for 10 kilometers (inclusive), and for the part above 10 kilometers, you can take 5 kilometers for each additional *yuan*. Use the municipal transportation card to swipe the card to take city public trams, and get 50% off for ordinary cards and 75% off for student cards on sections within the city; 20% off for sections outside the city.

zuò chū zū chē
坐出租车
Taking a taxi

核心句子 (Kernel Sentence)

nín yào qù nǎr
1. 您要去哪儿？

Where are you going?

出租车司机通常用这个问句询问乘客要去的目的地。乘客可以直接报地名作为回答，也可以提前把地名写下来，然后给司机看，或者直接说"去这儿"。

Taxi drivers usually use this question to ask passengers about their destination. Passengers can answer by quoting the place name. You can also write down the place name in advance and show it to the driver, or just say "qù zhèr ".

2. má fan nín kuài yì diǎnr , wǒ yào gǎn huǒ chē.
   麻烦您快一点儿，我要赶火车。

   Please hurry up, I have a train to catch.

"赶火车"里的"赶"为动词，意思是加快速度，不要错过时间。还可以用在"赶飞机"里。

The verb "gǎn" in "gǎn huǒ chē" means to speed up, not to miss time. You can also use it to catch a plane（gǎn fēi jī）.

3. nǐ yào zài nǎr xià chē?
   你要在哪儿下车？

   Where do you want to get off?

出租车接送乘客时，一般只能停在允许停靠的地方，不可以随便停放。一些没有表示禁止停车的地点也可以临时停放。

When taxis pick up and drop off passengers, they can only park where they are allowed, and they can't park at will. Some places that do not indicate no parking can also be temporarily parked.

实用场景（The Practical Situation）

» 1. 坐出租车 Taking a taxi

A：nín yào qù nǎr ?
您要去哪儿？

Where are you going?

B：qù wàn dá.
去万达。

Wanda.

A：**hǎo de．chē liàng qǐ bù，qǐng jì hǎo ān quán dài．**
好的。车辆起步，请系好安全带。

OK. Please fasten your seat belt as the vehicle starts.

B：**qù wàn dá duō shǎo qián？**
去万达多少钱？

How much is it to Wanda?

A：**nín fàng xīn，wǒ gěi nín dǎ biǎo．**
您放心，我给您打表。

Don't worry, I'll give you the meter.

2. 去高铁站 Going to the high-speed train station

A：**shī fu，wǒ yào qù gāo tiě zhàn．**
师傅，我要去高铁站。

Shifu, I'm going to the high-speed train station.

B：**hǎo lei．**
好嘞。

Okay.

A：**má fan nín kuài yì diǎnr，wǒ yào gǎn huǒ chē．**
麻烦您快一点儿，我要赶火车。

Please hurry up, I have a train to catch.

B：**hǎo de．shí wǔ fēn zhōng kě yǐ dào．**
好的。十五分钟可以到。

OK. You can be there in fifteen minutes.

3. 付车费 Paying the fare

A：**wàn dá dào le．nǐ zài nǎr xià chē？**
万达到了。你在哪儿下车？

Wanda arrived. Where do you get off?

B：就在前面那个路口吧，多少钱？

Just around the corner ahead. How much is it?

A：12 元。

12 yuan.

B：好的，我用支付宝付钱。

OK, I'll pay with Alipay.

核心词汇（Key Words）

序号	词语	拼音	翻译
1	安全带	ān quán dài	seat belt
2	行程表	xíng chéng biǎo	schedule
3	出租车	chū zū chē	taxi
4	高铁站	gāo tiě zhàn	high-speed railway station
5	支付	zhī fù	pay

你知道吗？—— 关于出租车（Do you know?—— Something about taxi）

乘坐出租车一般都要让司机打表，到达目的地之后按照计费表显示的金额付费。一般来说，夜间乘车价格要比白天贵一些。可通过拍照的方式记住车牌号码，万一下车后忘记拿东西，这时候可以通过车牌号到出租车公司等查找司机信息，然后找回丢失的东西。

Taxis are usually metered by the driver and paid according to the amount shown in the meter when arriving at the destination.In general, it is more expensive to travel at night than during the day. You can remember the license plate number by taking a photo. In case you forget to take something after getting off the taxis, you can go to a taxi company to find the driver's information through the license plate number and then retrieve the lost item.

坐地铁
Taking the subway

核心句子 (Kernel Sentence)

1. 最近的地铁站在哪儿？

Where is the nearest subway station?

2. 你可以在售票窗口或者自动售票机上买票。

You can buy tickets at the ticket window or the machine.

地铁站都设有售票窗口，有工作人员卖票，也可以去自动售票机买票。买票前先准备好1元硬币或者5元、10元纸币。

Subway stations have ticket windows, there are staff to sell tickets. You can also go to the vending machine to buy tickets. You'd better prepare 1 *yuan* coins or 5 *yuan* and 10 *yuan* bills before buying a ticket.

3. 请问我要去世纪公园应该坐几号线？

Could you tell me which line I should take to go to Century Park?

这里的"线"是路线的意思。如果想要表达地铁线路名称，可用这样的格式"数字+号+线"，如1号线、2号线。也可以另一种格式"地名+

四、出行

线"，如大兴线。

The word "xiàn" here means route. If you want to express the route of the subway, you can use the format "number +hào + xiàn", such as 1 hào xiàn 、2 hào xiàn (Line 1, Line 2).Another format "place name + xiàn" can also be used, such as dà xīng xiàn (Daxing Line) .

实用场景（The Practical Situation）

» 1. 地铁站在哪？ where is the subway station?

A：<ruby>请问<rt>qǐng wèn</rt></ruby>，<ruby>最近的地铁站在哪儿<rt>zuì jìn de dì tiě zhàn zài nǎr</rt></ruby>？

Excuse me, where is the nearest subway station?

B：<ruby>沿着这条路一直往前走<rt>yán zhe zhè tiáo lù yī zhí wǎng qián zǒu</rt></ruby>，<ruby>你会看到地铁站入口的标志<rt>nǐ huì kàn dào dì tiě zhàn rù kǒu de biāo zhì</rt></ruby>。

Go straight along this road and you'll see the sign for the entrance of the subway station.

A：<ruby>好的，谢谢<rt>hǎo de, xiè xie</rt></ruby>。

OK, thank you.

» 2. 购买地铁票 Buying subway tickets

A：<ruby>地铁票在哪里买<rt>dì tiě piào zài nǎ lǐ mǎi</rt></ruby>，<ruby>你知道吗<rt>nǐ zhī dào ma</rt></ruby>？

Do you know where to get a subway ticket?

B：<ruby>你可以在售票窗口或者自动售票机上买票<rt>nǐ kě yǐ zài shòu piào chuāng kǒu huò zhě zì dòng shòu piào jī shàng mǎi piào</rt></ruby>。

You can buy tickets at the ticket window or the machine.

A：大概多少钱一张票？我需要准备零钱吗？

How much is a ticket? Do I need any change?

B：起始票是3元，乘坐路程越远票价越高。需要自备零钱。

The ticket starts at 3 *yuan*, and the farther you travel, the higher the fare. You need to bring your own change.

3. 地铁路线 Subway route

A：请问我要去世纪公园应该坐几号线？

Could you tell me which line I should take to go to Century Park?

B：不好意思，我也不清楚。你可以看看那边墙上的地铁线路图。

I'm sorry, I don't know. You can look at the subway map on the wall over there.

4. 地铁坐反了 Taking the subway in the wrong direction

A：这不是开往世纪公园方向的，你应该是地铁坐反了方向。

This is not going to Century Park. You must have taken the subway in the wrong direction.

B：啊！那怎么办？我需要出去再重新买票吗？

Ah! What to do now? Do I need to go out and buy a new ticket?

四、出　行

A： nǐ zài xià yí zhàn xià chē， chóng xīn chéng zuò zhàn tái duì miàn de dì tiě jiù
你在下一站下车，重新乘坐站台对面的地铁就
xíng le， bù xū yào chū zhàn huàn chéng。
行了，不需要出站换乘。

You can get off at the next stop and take the subway opposite the platform again. There is no need to go out and change.

核心词汇（Key Words）

序号	词语	拼音	翻译
1	地铁站	dì tiě zhàn	subway station
2	入口	rù kǒu	entrance
3	地铁票	dì tiě piào	subway ticket
4	售票窗口	shòu piào chuāng kǒu	ticket window
5	自动售票机	zì dòng shòu piào jī	automatic ticket machine
6	起始票	qǐ shǐ piào	starting ticket
7	2号线	2 hào xiàn	Line 2
8	线路图	xiàn lù tú	circuit diagram
9	站台	zhàn tái	platform
10	换乘	huàn chéng	to transfer

你知道吗？——地铁坐反了方向怎么办？（Do you know?——What should I do if I take the subway in the wrong direction?）

乘坐地铁很容易坐反方向。首先你需要确定乘坐的是几号线，然后确定自己要去的站在线路上哪个方向。进入地铁站候车区，候车区上方会有液晶显示器告诉我们下一站是哪里，同时也会有语音播报。看准了自己的方向再上车，不要一看见地铁来了，就慌忙上车。一般情况下，地铁站台对面就是反方向的列车轨道，如果发现地铁坐反了，不必出站换乘，找到反向列车站台上车就行了。

It's easy to go the wrong way on the subway.First you need to determine which line you are taking, and then determine which direction on the line you want to go to.When we enter the waiting area of the subway station, there will be a liquid crystal display above the waiting area to tell us where the next stop is, and there will also be a voice broadcast.Check your direction before getting on the train. Don't rush on the train as soon as you see the train coming.Normally, the opposite of a subway platform is a train track in the opposite direction.If you find yourself on the wrong side of the train, you don't have to leave the station to change, just find the opposite train platform and get on.

zuò gāo tiě
坐 高 铁
Taking the high-speed train

核心句子（Kernel Sentence）

mǎi yì zhāng míng tiān qù shàng hǎi de piào.
1. 买 一 张 明 天 去 上 海 的 票。

A ticket to Shanghai for tomorrow.

同类句型替换：Substitution of similar sentence patterns:

mǎi yì zhāng hòu tiān qù běi jīng de piào.
买 一 张 后 天 去 北 京 的 票。 A ticket to Beijing the day after tomorrow.

mǎi liǎng zhāng míng tiān qù shàng hǎi de piào.
买 两 张 明 天 去 上 海 的 票。 Two tickets to Shanghai tomorrow.

qù gāo tiě zhàn huò zhě zài shǒu jī App shàng mǎi.
2. 去 高 铁 站 或 者 在 手 机 App 上 买。

Go to a high-speed train station or buy it on a mobile App.

火车票购票有两种方法。方法一，线上购买。在中国铁路局的官方App铁路12306上购买。方法二，直接拿上自己的有效证件去火车站的售票窗口购买。

There are two ways to buy train tickets. Method 1: Buy online. Buy it on the official App Railway 12306 of China Railway Administration. Method 2: Take your valid certificate directly and go to the ticket window of the railway station to buy it.

qǐng wèn cān chē zài jǐ hào chē xiāng?

3. 请问餐车在几号车厢?

Which compartment is the dining car, please?

中国火车可以分为高速动车组（G）、城际高速（C）、动车组（D）、直达特快旅客列车（Z）、特快旅客列车（T）、快速旅客列车（K）、普通百旅客列车（四位数字车次）、旅游列车（Y）、临时旅客列车（L）、通勤列车。

Chinese trains can be divided into high-speed EMUs (G), intercity high-speed rail(C), EMUs (D), direct express passenger trains (Z), express passenger trains (T), rapid passenger trains (K), and ordinary passenger trains. (four-digit number of trains), tourist train (Y), temporary passenger train (L), commuter train.

实用场景（The Practical Situation）

» 1. 买火车票 Buying train tickets

mǎi yì zhāng míng tiān qù shàng hǎi de piào.
B：买一张明天去上海的票。

A ticket to Shanghai for tomorrow.

hǎo de, yī děng zuò hé èr děng zuò, nín yào nǎ yì zhǒng?
A：好的，一等座和二等座，您要哪一种？

OK, first class and second class. Which would you like?

èr děng zuò.
B：二等座。

Second class.

221 yuán. zhè shì nín de piào, qǐng ná hǎo.
A：221元。这是您的票，请拿好。

221 *yuan*. Here are your tickets, please.

B：<ruby>谢<rt>xiè</rt></ruby> <ruby>谢<rt>xie</rt></ruby>！

Thanks.

» 2. 怎么去上海？How to get to shanghai?

A：<ruby>放<rt>fàng</rt></ruby> <ruby>假<rt>jià</rt></ruby> <ruby>了<rt>le</rt></ruby> <ruby>你<rt>nǐ</rt></ruby> <ruby>要<rt>yào</rt></ruby> <ruby>去<rt>qù</rt></ruby> <ruby>哪儿<rt>nǎr</rt></ruby> <ruby>玩<rt>wán</rt></ruby>？

Where are you going for your holiday?

B：<ruby>我<rt>wǒ</rt></ruby> <ruby>想<rt>xiǎng</rt></ruby> <ruby>去<rt>qù</rt></ruby> <ruby>上海<rt>shàng hǎi</rt></ruby> <ruby>旅<rt>lǚ</rt></ruby> <ruby>游<rt>yóu</rt></ruby>。

I want to travel to Shanghai.

A：<ruby>上海<rt>shàng hǎi</rt></ruby> <ruby>很<rt>hěn</rt></ruby> <ruby>远<rt>yuǎn</rt></ruby>，<ruby>你<rt>nǐ</rt></ruby> <ruby>怎么<rt>zěn me</rt></ruby> <ruby>去<rt>qù</rt></ruby> <ruby>呢<rt>ne</rt></ruby>？

Shanghai is very far away. How can you get there?

B：<ruby>坐<rt>zuò</rt></ruby> <ruby>高铁<rt>gāo tiě</rt></ruby>，4 <ruby>个<rt>gè</rt></ruby> <ruby>小时<rt>xiǎo shí</rt></ruby> <ruby>就<rt>jiù</rt></ruby> <ruby>能<rt>néng</rt></ruby> <ruby>到<rt>dào</rt></ruby>。

It takes four hours by high-speed train.

A：<ruby>去<rt>qù</rt></ruby> <ruby>哪儿<rt>nǎr</rt></ruby> <ruby>买<rt>mǎi</rt></ruby> <ruby>票<rt>piào</rt></ruby> <ruby>呢<rt>ne</rt></ruby>？

Where can I get a ticket?

B：<ruby>去<rt>qù</rt></ruby> <ruby>高铁<rt>gāo tiě</rt></ruby> <ruby>站<rt>zhàn</rt></ruby> <ruby>或者<rt>huò zhě</rt></ruby> <ruby>就<rt>jiù</rt></ruby> <ruby>在<rt>zài</rt></ruby> <ruby>手机<rt>shǒu jī</rt></ruby> App <ruby>上<rt>shàng</rt></ruby> <ruby>买<rt>mǎi</rt></ruby>。

Go to a high-speed train station or just buy it on a mobile App.

» 3. 火车用餐 Train meal

A：<ruby>请<rt>qǐng</rt></ruby> <ruby>问<rt>wèn</rt></ruby> <ruby>餐<rt>cān</rt></ruby> <ruby>车<rt>chē</rt></ruby> <ruby>在<rt>zài</rt></ruby> <ruby>几<rt>jǐ</rt></ruby> <ruby>号<rt>hào</rt></ruby> <ruby>车<rt>chē</rt></ruby> <ruby>厢<rt>xiāng</rt></ruby>？

Which compartment is the dining car, please?

B：5 号车厢。等一会儿列车员会推车来卖食物的，你也可以就在座位这儿等。

Car No. 5. The conductor will bring the cart to sell food later, or you can wait right here at your seat.

A：哦，好的。

Oh, good.

核心词汇（Key Words）

序号	词语	拼音	翻译
1	明天	míng tiān	tomorrow
2	火车票	huǒ chē piào	train ticket
3	一等座	yī děng zuò	first class
4	二等座	èr děng zuò	second class
5	硬座	yìng zuò	hard seat
6	卧铺	wò pù	sleeper
7	无座	wú zuò	no seat
8	餐车	cān chē	dining car

你知道吗？—— 如何在手机上购买火车票？（Do you know?—— How to buy train tickets on mobile phones?）

　　中国高速铁路是当代中国一类重要的交通基础设施。中国高铁座位分为商务座、一等座、二等座。票价不一样，舒适程度也不一样。一般情况下，我们可以去高铁站的售票处购买车票。但是如果你想更方便、更快捷，就可以用手机 App 来购买火车票。

　　China Railway Highspeed is an important kind of transportation infrastructure in contemporary China.China's high-speed rail seats are divided into business, first class and second class. The price of tickets varies, as does the comfort level.In general, we can go to the ticket office of the high-speed railway station to buy tickets. But if you want to make it easier and faster, you can use the mobile App to buy train tickets.

铁路官方售票网站12306推出英文版（www.12306.cn/en）。网站提供注册、登录、单程购票、改签、变更到站、退票、订单查询等功能。

The official railway ticketing website 12306 has launched an English version (www.12306.cn/en). The website provides registration, login, one-way ticket purchase, change, change to the station, refund, order query and other functions.

目前英文版只支持有效外国护照注册，而国内高铁和普速列车的电子客票系统仅支持中国身份证和中国护照，外国乘客暂无法直接刷外国护照进站，需提前打印购票信息单，走人工通道核验。

At present, the English version only supports valid foreign passport registration, while the e-ticket system of domestic high-speed trains and ordinary trains only supports Chinese ID card and Chinese passport. Foreign passengers cannot directly brush their foreign passports to enter the station. They need to print the ticket information form in advance and go through the manual channel for verification.

12306英文版网站支持多种支付方式，除了中文版现有支付方式（各大银行、支付宝、微信等）之外，还支持VISA、MasterCard、JCB、Diners四大国际卡组织，相关车票展示和交易均按人民币价格处理，通过中行完成国际卡支付。

12306 English version website supports a variety of payment methods. In addition to the existing Chinese version payment methods(major banks, Alipay, wechat, etc.), it also supports the VISA, MasterCard, JCB, Diners four international card organizations. Relevant ticket display and transaction are processed according to the price of RMB, and the international card payment is completed through the Bank of China.

四、出行

同时，12306还配套推出了英语电话客服服务（+86 21 12306）。12306英文版终于上线了，它可以为外国乘客提供更多方便。

At the same time, 12306 also launched supporting English telephone customer service (+86 21 12306). The English version of 12306 is finally online, which can provide more convenience for foreign passengers.

注：参考新浪新闻
https://news.sina.com.cn/s/2020-11-27/doc-iiznctke3648416.shtml。

坐飞机
Taking a plane

核心句子（Kernel Sentence）

1. 我想现在预订往返机票，比较划算。
   wǒ xiǎng xiàn zài yù dìng wǎng fǎn jī piào, bǐ jiào huá suàn.

   I want to book a round-trip ticket now. It's cheaper.

   "预订"意思是提前订购。"往返机票"也叫"双程机票"，就是去的机票和回的机票。如果您的行程还没有确定，那么要谨慎订购特价往返机票。大多数情况下特价往返机票是不可改签、不可退票的。

   "Yù dìng" means ordering in advance. "wǎng fǎn jī piào" is also called "shuāng chéng jī piào", that is, the ticket to go and the ticket to return. If your itinerary has not yet been determined, you should carefully order special round-trip air tickets. In most cases, the special round-trip air tickets cannot be changed or refunded.

2. 我想订一张2月13号去哈尔滨的机票。
   wǒ xiǎng dìng yī zhāng 2 yuè 13 hào qù hā ěr bīn de jī piào.

   I want to book a ticket to Harbin on February 13th.

如果你想表达"买什么地方的飞机票",就可以用"去+地方+机票"这样的格式。如果想说明时间,就把具体时间放在前面。

If you want to express "where do you want to fly to", you can use the format of "qù+place+jī piào". If you want to explain the time, put the specific time first.

3. 请问您要喝点什么?
   qǐng wèn nín yào hē diǎn shén me

What would you like to drink?

当飞机稳定地进入飞行状态之后,空姐会推一个小车在机舱内询问乘客是否需要饮品,如果你需要的话直接和空姐说就可以了。一般有饮料、牛奶、咖啡和矿泉水。

When the plane enters the flight state stably, the stewardess will push a small car in the cabin to ask the passengers if they need drinks. If you need drinks, just tell the stewardess directly. There are usually drinks, milk, coffee and mineral water.

☞ **实用场景**(The Practical Situation)

» 1. 坐飞机出去旅游 Travelling by plane

A:寒假你要出去旅游?
   hán jià nǐ yào chū qù lǚ yóu

Are you going to travel in winter vacation?

B:是的。我打算去哈尔滨玩一玩。
   shì de. wǒ dǎ suan qù hā ěr bīn wán yi wán

Yes. I'm going to Harbin for a visit.

A:你最好坐飞机去,春运期间,火车票可难买了,车上人还特别多。
   nǐ zuì hǎo zuò fēi jī qù, chūn yùn qī jiān, huǒ chē piào kě nán mǎi le, chē shàng rén hái tè bié duō.

You'd better go by air. It's hard to get train tickets during the Spring Festival travel season and there are too many people on the train.

· 102 ·

B：shì de, wǒ xiǎng xiàn zài jiù yù dìng wǎng fǎn jī piào, bǐ jiào huá suàn.
是的，我想现在就预订往返机票，比较划算。

Yes, I'd like to book a round-trip ticket now. It's cheaper.

» 2. 预订飞机票 Booking airline tickets

A：wǒ xiǎng dìng yì zhāng 2 yuè 13 hào qù hā ěr bīn de jī piào.
我想订一张2月13号去哈尔滨的机票。

I'd like to book a ticket to Harbin on February 13th.

B：dān chéng hái shì wǎng fǎn?
单程还是往返？

One way or round-trip ticket?

A：wǎng fǎn, 2 yuè 20 fǎn huí.
往返，2月20返回。

Round-trip, I will return on February 20.

B：hǎo de, jīng jì cāng xíng ma?
好的，经济舱行吗？

OK. Is economy class all right?

A：xíng. yǒu kào chuāng de wèi zi ma?
行。有靠窗的位子吗？

OK. Is there a seat by the window.

» 3. 飞机用餐 In-flight meal

A：qǐng wèn nín yào hē diǎn shén me? yǒu kā fēi、niú nǎi、kuàng quán shuǐ děng.
请问您要喝点什么？有咖啡、牛奶、矿泉水等。

What would you like to drink? We have coffee, milk, mineral water and so on.

B：gěi wǒ yì bēi niú nǎi.
给我一杯牛奶。

Give me a glass of milk.

· 103 ·

A：好的。请问还需要别的吗？
hǎo de. qǐng wèn hái xū yào bié de ma?

OK.Do you need anything else?

B：如果有吃的东西，可以拿一点过来。肚子有点饿了。
rú guǒ yǒu chī de dōng xi, kě yǐ ná yì diǎn guò lai. dù zi yǒu diǎn è le.

If you have something to eat, you can bring some. I'm a little hungry.

核心词汇（Key Words）

序号	词语	拼音	翻译
1	预订	yù dìng	booking
2	划算	huá suàn	cost-effective
3	往返	wǎng fǎn	round trip
4	机票	jī piào	the air ticket
5	春运	chūn yùn	Spring Festival travel season
6	经济舱	jīng jì cāng	economy class
7	头等舱	tóu děng cāng	first class

你知道吗？——春运（Do you know?—— The Spring Festival transport season）

春运，即春节运输，是中国在农历春节前后发生的一种大规模的高交通运输压力的现象。外出务工、求学的人都集中在春节期间返乡，形成了堪称"全球罕见的人口流动"的春运。每年农历腊月十五至次年正月廿五，共40天左右。在这40天左右的时间里，有30多亿人次的人口流动，占世界人口的1/2，相当于全国人民进行两次大迁移。春运期间多数地区都采取了提前预订的方式。

Spring Festival transport is a large-scale phenomenon of high traffic and transport

四、出行

pressure occurring around the Lunar New Year in China. People who go out for work or study all go back to their hometowns during the Spring Festival, forming the Spring Festival transportation that can be called "rare population flow in the world". It lasts about 40 days from the 15th day of the 12th lunar month to the 25th day of the following year.During the 40-day period, more than 3 billion people moved, accounting for half of the world's population, which is equivalent to two major migrations of people in China. During the Spring Festival travel rush, most regions have adopted advance booking.

订酒店房间
Booking a hotel room

核心句子 (Kernel Sentence)

1. 我想预订一个标间。
   wǒ xiǎng yù dìng yí gè biāo jiān.

   I'd like to reserve a standard room.

   一般来说，标间是两张标准单人床的房间，这是最普遍的房型。另外还有单人间、大床房、豪华标间、行政套房、高级套房、豪华套房、总统套房等。

   Generally speaking, a standard room is a room with two standard twin beds. This is the most common type of room. In addition, there are single room, double room, deluxe standard room, executive suite, senior suite, deluxe suite, presidential suite and so on.

2. 等一会儿订房信息会发送到您手机上，请注意查收。
   děng yí huìr dìng fáng xìn xī huì fā sòng dào nín shǒu jī shàng, qǐng zhù yì chá shōu.

   The reservation information will be sent to your phone later, please check it.

· 105 ·

一般来说订房订单确认后，酒店会发送确认短信到订单中的联系人手机。如果30分钟内还没有收到确认短信，就需要打电话给酒店确认一下房间是否预订成功。

Generally speaking, after the reservation order is confirmed, the hotel will send a confirmation message to the contact person's mobile phone in the order. If you haven't received the confirmation message within 30 minutes, you need to call the hotel to confirm whether the room was booked successfully.

3. 请问你们有没有接机服务？
   qǐngwèn nǐ men yǒu méi yǒu jiē jī fú wù？

Do you have airport pick-up service?

"接机服务"的意思是在乘客下飞机之后，会有专门的接机人员来迎接，将乘客接到指定的下榻酒店。接机服务一般都是要收费的，也不是所有酒店都提供这样的服务。需要您提前打电话跟酒店确认。

"jiē jī fú wù" means that after passengers get off the plane, there will be a special pick-up person to meet them and pick them up to the designated hotel. Pick-up service is generally charged, and not all hotels provide such service. You need to call the hotel in advance to confirm.

☞ **实用场景**（The Practical Situation）

» 1. 预订房间 Booking a room

A：我想预订一个标间。
   wǒ xiǎng yù dìng yí gè biāo jiān.

I'd like to reserve a standard room.

B：请问您什么时间入住呢？
   qǐng wèn nín shén me shí jiān rù zhù ne？

When would you like to check in?

A：<ruby>下<rt>xià</rt></ruby> <ruby>周<rt>zhōu</rt></ruby> <ruby>三<rt>sān</rt></ruby>。

Next Wednesday.

B：<ruby>好<rt>hǎo</rt></ruby> <ruby>的<rt>de</rt></ruby>。<ruby>我<rt>wǒ</rt></ruby> <ruby>们<rt>men</rt></ruby> <ruby>酒<rt>jiǔ</rt></ruby> <ruby>店<rt>diàn</rt></ruby> <ruby>有<rt>yǒu</rt></ruby> <ruby>不<rt>bù</rt></ruby> <ruby>同<rt>tóng</rt></ruby> <ruby>规<rt>guī</rt></ruby> <ruby>格<rt>gé</rt></ruby> <ruby>的<rt>de</rt></ruby> <ruby>房<rt>fáng</rt></ruby> <ruby>间<rt>jiān</rt></ruby>，<ruby>您<rt>nín</rt></ruby> <ruby>要<rt>yào</rt></ruby> <ruby>订<rt>dìng</rt></ruby> <ruby>哪<rt>nǎ</rt></ruby> <ruby>一<rt>yì</rt></ruby> <ruby>种<rt>zhǒng</rt></ruby>？

OK. Our hotel has different sizes of rooms, which one would you like to book?

A：<ruby>标<rt>biāo</rt></ruby> <ruby>间<rt>jiān</rt></ruby> <ruby>吧<rt>ba</rt></ruby>。

Standard rooms.

2. 预订房间 Booking a room

B：<ruby>请<rt>qǐng</rt></ruby> <ruby>报<rt>bào</rt></ruby> <ruby>一<rt>yí</rt></ruby> <ruby>下<rt>xià</rt></ruby> <ruby>您<rt>nín</rt></ruby> <ruby>的<rt>de</rt></ruby> <ruby>姓<rt>xìng</rt></ruby> <ruby>名<rt>míng</rt></ruby> <ruby>和<rt>hé</rt></ruby> <ruby>手<rt>shǒu</rt></ruby> <ruby>机<rt>jī</rt></ruby> <ruby>号<rt>hào</rt></ruby> <ruby>码<rt>mǎ</rt></ruby>。

May I have your name and mobile number, please?

A：<ruby>我<rt>wǒ</rt></ruby> <ruby>的<rt>de</rt></ruby> <ruby>名<rt>míng</rt></ruby> <ruby>字<rt>zi</rt></ruby> <ruby>是<rt>shì</rt></ruby> <ruby>王<rt>wáng</rt></ruby> <ruby>兵<rt>bīng</rt></ruby>。<ruby>电<rt>diàn</rt></ruby> <ruby>话<rt>huà</rt></ruby> <ruby>是<rt>shì</rt></ruby> 1 3 8……。

My name is Wang Bing. Phone number is 138... .

B：<ruby>好<rt>hǎo</rt></ruby> <ruby>的<rt>de</rt></ruby>，<ruby>已<rt>yǐ</rt></ruby> <ruby>经<rt>jīng</rt></ruby> <ruby>预<rt>yù</rt></ruby> <ruby>订<rt>dìng</rt></ruby> <ruby>成<rt>chéng</rt></ruby> <ruby>功<rt>gōng</rt></ruby> <ruby>了<rt>le</rt></ruby>。<ruby>等<rt>děng</rt></ruby> <ruby>一<rt>yí</rt></ruby> <ruby>会<rt>huì</rt></ruby> <ruby>儿<rt>r</rt></ruby> <ruby>订<rt>dìng</rt></ruby> <ruby>房<rt>fáng</rt></ruby> <ruby>信<rt>xìn</rt></ruby> <ruby>息<rt>xī</rt></ruby> <ruby>会<rt>huì</rt></ruby> <ruby>发<rt>fā</rt></ruby> <ruby>送<rt>sòng</rt></ruby> <ruby>到<rt>dào</rt></ruby> <ruby>您<rt>nín</rt></ruby> <ruby>手<rt>shǒu</rt></ruby> <ruby>机<rt>jī</rt></ruby> <ruby>上<rt>shàng</rt></ruby>，<ruby>请<rt>qǐng</rt></ruby> <ruby>注<rt>zhù</rt></ruby> <ruby>意<rt>yì</rt></ruby> <ruby>查<rt>chá</rt></ruby> <ruby>收<rt>shōu</rt></ruby>。

OK, the reservation has been made. The reservation information will be sent to your phone later, please check it.

3. 接机服务 Airport pick-up service

A：你好，我在你们酒店预订了一间房，请问你们有没有接机服务？
nǐ hǎo, wǒ zài nǐ men jiǔ diàn yù dìng le yì jiān fáng, qǐng wèn nǐ men yǒu méi yǒu jiē jī fú wù?

Hello, I have reserved a room in your hotel. Do you have airport pick-up service?

B：不好意思！我们酒店没有接机服务。您可以乘坐机场地铁，或者出租车来我们酒店。
bù hǎo yì si! wǒ men jiǔ diàn méi yǒu jiē jī fú wù. nín kě yǐ chéng zuò jī chǎng dì tiě, huò zhě chū zū chē lái wǒ men jiǔ diàn.

Excuse me! We don't have airport pick-up service in our hotel. You can take the airport subway or a taxi to our hotel.

核心词汇（Key Words）

序号	词语	拼音	翻译
1	标间	biāo jiān	standard room
2	套房	tào fáng	suite
3	大床房	dà chuáng fáng	big bed room
4	单人间	dān rén jiān	single room
5	预订	yù dìng	booking
6	预留	yù liú	reserved
7	取消	qǔ xiāo	cancel

你知道吗？—— 酒店预订需要注意哪些问题？（Do you know?—— What matters need to pay attention to about hotel booking?）

成功地预订酒店后，临时有事耽误入住时间，可打电话到酒店告知原因，让酒店保留房间。国内旅游地区的酒店在旺季、大型节假日的时候，

四、出 行

用房量是很紧张的，所以有出行安排的话需要提前预订。预订酒店不需要提供任何有效证件，只需要提供姓名和电话号码预订便可，入住酒店办理入住时需要提供有效证件，如身份证、护照等。

After booking a hotel successfully, if there is something to delay the check-in time, you can call the hotel to inform the reason and ask the hotel to keep the room. Hotel rooms in domestic tourist areas are very tight during peak seasons, large holidays. So you need to book in advance if you have travel plans. You don't need to provide any valid identification when you book a hotel. You just need to provide your name and telephone number. When checking into the hotel, you need to provide valid documents, such as ID card, passport, etc.

入住酒店
Check in hotel

☞ 核心句子（Kernel Sentence）

1. 您好，我要办理入住。
   nín hǎo, wǒ yào bàn lǐ rù zhù.

Hello, I'd like to check in, please.

入住手续在酒店前台办理即可。需要您拿着身份证或者护照，按照前台服务人员的要求办理入住手续。

Check-in is handled at the front desk of the hotel. You are required to take your ID card or passport and check in according to the requirements of the front desk service personnel.

2. 这是您的房卡和早餐券。
   zhè shì nín de fáng kǎ hé zǎo cān quàn.

Here is your room card and breakfast coupon.

· 109 ·

酒店订房时，如果房间带早餐，就可以凭房卡或者早餐券直接去酒店餐厅免费吃早餐。如果你预订的房间不带早餐，就没有免费的早餐可吃。一般，双人房有2张早餐券，单人房就只有1张。

When booking a hotel, if the room has breakfast, you can go directly to the hotel restaurant for free breakfast with your room card or breakfast voucher. If you book a room without breakfast, there is no free breakfast available. Generally, there are two breakfast vouchers in a double room, and only one in a single room.

3. 服务员，我房间的马桶有问题，你可以过来看看吗？

Waiter, there is something wrong with the toilet in my room. Can you come and have a look?

如果入住的酒店房间有设备或者物品损坏，只要你的理由正当，酒店一般都会给你更换房间。

If the equipment or articles in the hotel room are damaged, the hotel will change the room for you as long as your reasons are justified.

实用场景（The Practical Situation）

» 1. 办理入住 Check in

A: 您好，我要办理入住。

Hello, I'd like to check in, please.

B: 好的，请问您有预订吗？

OK, do you have a reservation?

四、出 行

A：有，叫王兵，电话是138……。

Yes, it's Wang Bing and the number is 138... .

B：请稍等。您在我们这里预订了一个标准间，对吗？

Please wait a moment. You have reserved a standard room with us, right?

» 2. 入住手续办好了 Check-in is done

A：请出示您的护照。入住手续已经办理好了，请您确认好了再签字。

Please show me your passport. The check-in has been completed. Please confirm before you sign.

B：好的，没问题。

Good, no problem.

A：这是您的房卡，房间是五楼的1502号。这是您的早餐券，早餐供应时间为早上7:00到9:30，早餐在二楼的西餐厅。

Here is your room card. It's room 1502 on the fifth floor. Here is your breakfast ticket. Breakfast is served from 7:00 to 9:30 in the morning. The breakfast is in the western restaurant on the second floor.

B：好的，谢谢！

OK, thank you.

· 111 ·

» 3. 房间有问题 Problem with the room

A：服务员，我房间的马桶有问题，你可以过来看看吗？
fú wù yuán, wǒ fáng jiān de mǎ tǒng yǒu wèn tí, nǐ kě yǐ guò lai kàn kan ma?

Waiter, there is something wrong with the toilet in my room. Can you come and have a look?

B：好的，哪个房间？
hǎo de, nǎ ge fáng jiān?

OK, which room?

A：1502。
1502.

1502.

B：很抱歉，马桶暂时修不好，可以为您换另一个房间吗？
hěn bào qiàn, mǎ tǒng zàn shí xiū bù hǎo, kě yǐ wéi nín huàn lìng yí gè fáng jiān ma?

I'm sorry. The toilet can't be fixed for now. Can I change another room for you?

☞ 核心词汇（Key Words）

序号	词语	拼音	翻译
1	入住	rù zhù	be opened for occupancy
2	房卡	fáng kǎ	room card
3	早餐券	zǎo cān quàn	breakfast voucher
4	前台电话	qián tái diàn huà	front desk telephone
5	叫醒服务	jiào xǐng fú wù	wake-up service
6	马桶	mǎ tǒng	toilet
7	浴缸	yù gāng	bathtub

续表

8	水龙头	shuǐ lóng tóu	water tap
9	灯	dēng	lamp
10	空调	kōng tiáo	air conditioning
11	电视	diàn shì	TV
12	烧水壶	shāo shuǐ hú	kettle

你知道吗？—— 民宿（Do you know?—— Homestay）

民宿不同于传统的饭店旅馆，它没有高级奢华的设施，但它能让人体验当地风情、体验有别于城市的生活。随着人们的旅行观念和出游方式的变化，旅游消费者已不再满足于走马观花式的旅游，以民宿为核心的住民居、吃特色餐、搭便车、利用本地人伴游的深度休闲体验游模式越来越受青睐。原来大部分人出行都选择住酒店，但是现在民宿被大众所接受，乡村的生活方式被越来越多的人所了解和接受。

Unlike traditional hotels, homestays do not have high level and luxury facilities, but they allow people to experience the local customs and experience the life different from the city.With the change of people's travel concept and travel mode, tourism consumers are no longer satisfied with the tourism of a quick glance, and the deep leisure experience mode of living in residential houses, eating special meals, hitchhiking and using local companions is becoming more and more popular.Originally most people choose to live in hotels, but now homestay is accepted by the public.The way of life in the country is understood and accepted by more and more people.

五、生活娱乐
Life and Entertainment

看电影
Seeing a movie

> 核心句子 (Kernel Sentence)

1. 你喜欢什么类型的电影？
nǐ xǐ huan shén me lèi xíng de diàn yǐng?

What kind of movies do you like?

中国电影有很多类型，其中包含动作片、战争片、剧情片、故事片、喜剧片等等。

There are many types of Chinese films, including action films, war films, feature films, comedies and so on.

2. 我昨天看了一部喜剧片，可好看了！
wǒ zuó tiān kàn le yí bù xǐ jù piàn, kě hǎo kàn le!

I watched a comedy yesterday, it was so good!

"可好看"的意思是非常好看、特别好看。"可+形容词"可表示程度深，口语里常用。

"kě hǎo kàn" means very good-looking and particularly good-looking. "kě+Adjective" can express deeply and is commonly used in spOKen Chinese.

五、生活娱乐

3．<ruby>我们<rt>wǒ men</rt></ruby> <ruby>去<rt>qù</rt></ruby> <ruby>哪儿<rt>nǎr</rt></ruby> <ruby>看电影<rt>kàn diànyǐng</rt></ruby> <ruby>啊<rt>a</rt></ruby>？

Where shall we go to see the movie?

实用场景（The Practical Situation）

1. 去看电影 Going to the movies

A：<ruby>明天<rt>míng tiān</rt></ruby> <ruby>是<rt>shì</rt></ruby> <ruby>大年初一<rt>dà nián chū yī</rt></ruby>，<ruby>你<rt>nǐ</rt></ruby> <ruby>打算<rt>dǎ suàn</rt></ruby> <ruby>干什么<rt>gàn shén me</rt></ruby>？

Tomorrow is New Year's day. What are you going to do?

B：<ruby>我<rt>wǒ</rt></ruby> <ruby>还<rt>hái</rt></ruby> <ruby>没<rt>méi</rt></ruby> <ruby>想好<rt>xiǎng hǎo</rt></ruby>，<ruby>你<rt>nǐ</rt></ruby> <ruby>呢<rt>ne</rt></ruby>？

I haven't decided yet. What about you?

A：<ruby>明天<rt>míng tiān</rt></ruby> <ruby>有<rt>yǒu</rt></ruby> <ruby>好几部<rt>hǎo jǐ bù</rt></ruby> <ruby>贺岁片<rt>hè suì piàn</rt></ruby> <ruby>要<rt>yào</rt></ruby> <ruby>上映<rt>shàngyìng</rt></ruby>，<ruby>我们<rt>wǒ men</rt></ruby> <ruby>去<rt>qù</rt></ruby> <ruby>看看<rt>kàn kan</rt></ruby> <ruby>呗<rt>bei</rt></ruby>？

There are several New Year films to be shown tomorrow. Shall we go and see them?

B：<ruby>好呀<rt>hǎo ya</rt></ruby>！<ruby>有什么<rt>yǒu shén me</rt></ruby> <ruby>电影<rt>diànyǐng</rt></ruby>？

Good! What movies are?

A：<ruby>我看看<rt>wǒ kàn kan</rt></ruby>。<ruby>有<rt>yǒu</rt></ruby> <ruby>喜剧片<rt>xǐ jù piàn</rt></ruby>、<ruby>爱情片<rt>ài qíng piàn</rt></ruby>，<ruby>还有<rt>hái yǒu</rt></ruby> <ruby>动作片<rt>dòng zuò piàn</rt></ruby>。

Let me see. There are comedies, romances and action movies.

B：<ruby>你<rt>nǐ</rt></ruby> <ruby>喜欢<rt>xǐ huan</rt></ruby> <ruby>什么<rt>shén me</rt></ruby> <ruby>类型<rt>lèi xíng</rt></ruby> <ruby>的<rt>de</rt></ruby> <ruby>电影<rt>diànyǐng</rt></ruby>？

What kind of movies do you like?

115

» 2. 看了一部喜剧片 I watched a comedy

A：_{wǒ zuó tiān kàn le yí bù xǐ jù piàn, kě hǎo kàn le!}
我昨天看了一部喜剧片，可好看了！

I watched a comedy yesterday, it was so good!

B：_{nǐ yě xǐ huan kàn xǐ jù piàn ma?}
你也喜欢看喜剧片吗？

Do you like watching comedies, too?

A：是呀。主演是中国著名的喜剧演员，演得真不错！你真应该去看看。

Yeah. The star is a famous Chinese comedian, and he did a great job! You really should see it.

» 3. 买电影票 Buying movie tickets

A：我们去哪儿看电影啊？

Where shall we go to see the movie?

B：万达吧。看完电影还可以在那儿吃饭。

Wanda. We can eat there after the movie.

B：好的，那赶快在手机上买票吧，挑个好场次和座位。

OK.Then let's buy tickets on the phone quickly, so that we can choose a good show and seat.

五、生活娱乐

☞ 核心词汇（Key Words）

序号	词语	拼音	翻译
1	电影	diàn yǐng	film
2	电影院	diàn yǐng yuàn	cinema
3	去哪儿	qù nǎr	Where to go?
4	贺岁片	hè suì piàn	Chinese New Year film
5	上映	shàng yìng	release/show
6	喜剧演员	xǐ jù yǎn yuán	comedian
7	电影票	diàn yǐng piào	movie ticket
8	座位	zuò wèi	seat
9	场次	chǎng cì	session

☞ 你知道吗？——贺岁片（Do you know?—— New Year Movies）

贺岁片是指在元旦、春节期间上映的电影。寻求欢乐和放松，是观众逢年过节，尤其是春节期间普遍的心理需求。这就决定了贺岁片的风格普遍是轻松的、幽默的，其具有强烈的观赏性和娱乐性。因此，其题材多与百姓节日期间喜庆、祝福的生活与习俗相关，形式多是娱乐性、消遣性较强的喜剧片和动作片。

——参考360百科"贺岁片"https://baike.so.com/doc/3202188-3374747.html

New Year films refer to films released during New Year's Day and Spring Festival. Seeking for joy and relaxation is a common psychological demand of audiences during festivals, especially the Spring Festival. This determines that the style of New Year films is generally relaxed, humorous, with strong ornamental and entertaining. Therefore, its themes are mostly related to people's happy and blessed life and customs during festivals, and its forms are mostly comedies and action movies with strong entertainment and recreational characteristics.

qù yín háng去 银 行
Go to the bank

> 核心句子（Kernel Sentence）

nǐ hǎo, wǒ yào huànqián.
1. 你好，我要换钱。

Hello, I'd like to change some money.

在中国可以换外币的银行有很多，最常见的就是中国工商银行、中国建设银行、中国银行、中国农业银行、交通银行。但是并不是所有的银行网点都能办理，有些城市只有特定的某个银行网点才能办理。因此，如果您持外币想前往银行兑换，最好先咨询清楚，不然白跑一趟。

There are many banks that can exchange foreign currency in China, the most common of which are Industrial and Commercial Bank of China, China Construction Bank, Bank of China, Agricultural Bank of China and Bank of Communications. However, not all bank outlets can handle it. In some cities, only a specific bank outlet can handle it. Therefore, if you want to go to the bank to exchange foreign currency, you'd better consult clearly first, or you'll make a vain trip.

wǒ xiǎng kāi tōng yí gè yín hángzhàng hù.
2. 我想开通一个银行账户。

I'd like to open a bank account.

如果外国人想在中国办理银行账户，必须携带护照、工作或者学习证明等必备资料去银行网点办理。不同银行之间存在差异，去之前最好电话咨询银行的客服人员，或者到银行网点咨询，做好充分的准备。

If foreigners want to apply for bank accounts in China, they must go to the bank outlets with passports, work or study certificates and other necessary information. There are differences between different banks, so it's best to consult the customer service staff of the bank by phone before going there, or go to the bank outlets for consultation and make full preparations.

3. 赶快拨打银行客服电话临时挂失。
gǎn kuài bō dǎ yín háng kè fú diàn huà lín shí guà shī

Call the bank customer service phone and report the loss temporarily.

如果银行卡不小心遗失了，马上拨打银行的客服电话，按照语音提示一步一步进行操作。

If the bank card is accidentally lost, immediately call the customer service number of the bank and follow the voice prompts to operate step by step.

☞ 实用场景（The Practical Situation）

» 1. 换钱 Changing money

A：你好，我要换钱。
（nǐ hǎo, wǒ yào huànqián.）

Hello, I'd like to change some money.

B：请问换什么钱？
（qǐng wèn huàn shén me qián?）

What kind of money do you want?

A：人民币。我要换200美元的人民币。
（rén mín bì. wǒ yào huàn 200 měi yuán de rén mín bì.）

Ren Min Bi. I'd like to change 200 US dollars into RMB.

B：好的，请把护照给我，再填一下这个单子。
（hǎo de, qǐng bǎ hù zhào gěi wǒ, zài tián yí xià zhè ge dān zi.）

OK, please give me your passport and fill out this slip.

A：好的。
（hǎo de.）

Okay.

· 119 ·

B：请在这里签字。这是您的护照和钱，请收好。

Please sign here. Here is your passport and money. Please keep them.

2. 开户 Opening an account

A：我想开通一个银行账户。

I'd like to open a bank account.

B：请把您的护照给我，并填写您面前的表格。

Please give me your passport and fill in the form in front of you.

A：好的。填好了。

OK. Filled out.

B：请您抬头看向左边的摄像头，我们需要采集比对您的面部信息，并录取指纹。

Please look up at the camera on the left, we need to collect and match your face, and take fingerprints.

A：好的。

Okay.

B：您要给银行卡设置一个六位数的密码，请在您面前的机器上输入。

You need to set up a six-digit password for your bank card. Please enter it in the machine in front of you.

A：好的。

Okay.

B：账户已经为您开通好了，这是您的银行卡和相关凭证，请拿好。您还可以在手机上下载App，用您的手机号注册并登录，可以在手机银行里完成转账、查账等业务。

The account has been opened for you. Here is your bank card and relevant certificates. Please take them. You can also download the App on your phone, register and log in with your phone number. You can transfer money and check accounts in mobile banking.

» 3. 银行卡挂失 Reporting loss of bank card

A：哎呀，我的银行卡丢了，怎么办？

Oh, I lost my bank card. What should I do?

B：赶快拨打银行客服电话临时挂失，一般临时挂失的有效期是5天。临时挂失后，你拿护照到银行办理正式挂失手续。正式挂失后一般需要等七天的时间，之后再拿护照和挂失证明到银行补办一张新的银行卡。

Call bank customer service phone to report loss temporarily as soon as possible, the validity period of temporary loss reporting is 5 days. After the temporary loss reporting, you take your passport to the bank to handle the formal loss reporting procedures. It generally takes seven days after the official loss report, and then a new bank card will be issued at the bank with the passport and the loss report certificate.

A：xiè xie nǐ！xìng kuī nǐ zhī dào zěn me guà shī.
谢谢你！幸亏你知道怎么挂失。

Thank you very much. Fortunately, you know how to report a lost bank card.

B：bú kè qi，shàng gè yuè wǒ de yín háng kǎ yě diū le.
不客气，上个月我的银行卡也丢了。

You're welcome. I lost my bank card last month, too.

核心词汇（Key Words）

序号	词语	拼音	翻译
1	换钱	huàn qián	change money
2	人民币	rén mín bì	RMB
3	美元	měi yuán	dollar
4	日元	rì yuán	Japanese yen
5	英镑	yīng bàng	pound
6	护照	hù zhào	passport
7	账号	zhàng hào	account number
8	信息采集	xìn xī cǎi jí	information acquisition
9	密码	mì mǎ	password
10	转账	zhuǎn zhàng	transfer
11	账单	zhàng dān	bill
12	挂失	guà shī	report the loss

你知道吗？——中国四大银行（Do you know?——China's Big Four Banks）

中国四大银行是指中国工商银行、中国农业银行、中国银行、中国建设银行，亦称中央四大行。

五、生活娱乐

中国工商银行（Industrial and Commercial Bank of China），简称ICBC，工行。客户服务与投诉热线：95588。

中国农业银行（Agricultural Bank of China），简称ABC，农行。客户服务与投诉热线：95599。

中国银行（Bank of China），简称BOC，中行。客户服务与投诉热线：95566。

中国建设银行（China Construction Bank），简称CCB，建行。客户服务与投诉热线：95533。

China's big four banks are Industrial and Commercial Bank of China, Agricultural Bank of China, Bank of China and China Construction Bank, also known as the four central banks.

Industrial and Commercial Bank of China referred to as ICBC, "gōng háng". Customer service and complaints hotline: 95588.

Agricultural Bank of China referred to as ABC, "nóng háng". Customer service and complaints hotline: 95599.

Bank of China referred to as BOC, "zhōng háng". Customer service and complaints hotline: 95566.

China Construction Bank referred to as CCB, "jiàn háng". Customer service and complaints hotline: 95533.

租 房
Renting an apartment

核心句子 (Kernel Sentence)

1. 可以在网上租，有专门的租房网站，也可以去找房产中介。

You can rent online, there are special rental websites, or you can go to a real estate agent.

租房的方式有很多，比较常见的是整租和合租。合租就是至少两人一起租住一间或一套住房，厨房、卫生间等共同使用。房屋的租金、电费、水费等费用由合租的几个人共同分摊。整租就是一个人租一套房子，不与其他人共住。租房产生的所有费用都由租房者一个人承担。

There are many ways to rent a house, and the common ones are whole rent and shared rent. Sharing means that at least two people rent one or a set of houses together, and the kitchen and bathroom are used together. The rent, electricity and water charges of the house are shared by several people sharing the house. Whole rent means that a person rents a house without sharing it with others. All expenses incurred in renting a house shall be borne by the renter alone.

2. 我想租一套一室一厅的公寓，要有厨房和卫生间。

I want to rent a one-bedroom apartment with a kitchen and a bathroom.

"室"就是"卧室"。"厅"就是"客厅""餐厅"。一般情况"一室一厅"

的意思是一个卧室一个客厅。另外，还有两室一厅，两室两厅。"两室一厅"就是两个卧室，一个客厅。"两室两厅"就是两个卧室，一个客厅，一个餐厅。一般套房都会默认一个厨房，一个卫生间，不会单独强调。但是，如果不止一个卫生间，就可以这么说"三室两厅一厨两卫"。

"shì" is "bedroom". "tīng" means "living room" and "dining room". Generally speaking, "yí shì yì tīng" means one bedroom and one living room. In addition, there are "liǎng shì yì tīng" and "liǎng shì liǎng tīng". "liǎng shì yì tīng" means two bedrooms and one living room. "liǎng shì liǎng tīng" means two bedrooms, one living room and one dining room. General suites will default to a kitchen and a bathroom, which will not be emphasized separately. However, if there is more than one bathroom, you can say "sān shì liǎng tīng yì chú liǎng wèi".

3. yí gè yuè 1 8 0 0，yā yī fù yī，bàn nián qǐ zū.
   一个月1800，押一付一，半年起租。

The rent is 1800 *yuan* a month, pay one month's rent and one month's deposit. Rental time at least six months.

"半年起租"指租房期限最少半年，一般来说，需要先缴纳两个月房租的钱，其中只算一个月的租金，另一个月的租金作为押金抵押给房东。

"bàn nián qǐ zū" means the rental term at least half a year. Generally speaking, you need to pay two months' rent in advance, of which only one month's rent is counted, and the other month's rent is used as a deposit to the landlord.

实用场景（The Practical Situation）

» 1. 怎么租房？How to rent a house?

A：wǒ xiǎng zài xiào wài zū gè gōng yù．nǐ zhī dào zěn me zū ma？
我想在校外租个公寓。你知道怎么租吗？

I want to rent an apartment off campus. Do you know how to rent it?

B：可以在网上租，有专门的租房网站，也可以去找房产中介。

You can rent online, there are special rental websites, or you can go to a real estate agent.

A：那你能陪我去中介看看吗？

Can you go to the agency with me?

B：可以。

OK.

2. 在房产中介 In a real estate agent

A：你好，是租房还是买房？

Hello, rent or buy?

B：我们想在附近租个公寓。

We want to rent an apartment nearby.

A：想要租多大的？一室一厅？还是两室一厅？

What size do you want? One room, one living room? Or two rooms and a living room?

B：一室一厅的吧。要有厨房和卫生间。

One room and one living room. There should be a kitchen and a bathroom.

五、生活娱乐

A：你看看这套房怎么样？就在旁边的小区，治安很好，房子在12楼，一室一厅，一厨一卫正合适。这是房间的照片，你看看。

How about this suite? The house is in the next neighborhood and the security is very good. It's on the 12th floor, with one bedroom, one living room, one kitchen and one bathroom. This is pictures of the room. Look at this.

B：能去房子看看吗？

Can we take a look at the house?

» 3. 谈论租金 Discussing rent

A：房子不错，租金多少？

It's a nice apartment. How much is the rent?

B：一个月1800，押一付一，半年起租。

The rent is 1800 *yuan* a month, pay one for one. Rental time at least six months.

A：这么贵啊！

It's so expensive!

B：这样的好房子一个月不到2000块，已经很便宜了，你在别处根本租不到的。

Such a good house is less than 2000 *yuan* a month, which is already a bargain. You can't get it anywhere else.

· 127 ·

A：那好吧。我们签个合同。
　　nà hǎo ba。wǒ men qiān gè hé tong。

That is all right. Let's sign a contract.

核心词汇（Key Words）

序号	词语	拼音	翻译
1	整租	zhěng zū	whole rent
2	合租	hé zū	flat sharing
3	公寓	gōng yù	apartment
4	房租	fáng zū	rent
5	水费	shuǐ fèi	water rate
6	电费	diàn fèi	power rate
7	厨房	chú fáng	kitchen
8	卫生间	wèi shēng jiān	toilet
9	餐厅	cān tīng	dining room
10	客厅	kè tīng	sitting room
11	卧室	wò shì	bedroom
12	押金	yā jīn	deposit
13	合同	hé tóng	contract

你知道吗？—— 租房的"押一付一"是什么意思？（Do you know?—— What does "pay one for one" mean？）

"押一付一"是承租方在支付第一个月的房租的同时还需再支付一个月的房租作为押金。一般出现在房屋租赁合同中，是用来保证其在租赁期间不会损坏房屋的设备。如果因个人原因造成房屋设备的损坏则保证金不予退还。当租赁期满时，出租方应将押金退还给租赁方，或者按照合同约定的期限返还。

"Pay one for one" is when the tenant pays the first month's rent in addition to

五、生活娱乐

another month's rent as a deposit.It is used to ensure that the tenant will not damage the house during the lease period.The deposit will not be refunded if the premises and equipment are damaged due to personal reasons.When the lease expires, the lessor shall return the deposit to the lessee, or according to the time limit agreed in the contract.

办理无线网络
bàn lǐ wú xiàn wǎng luò
Managing a wireless Network

核心句子（Kernel Sentence）

1. 你可以去中国电信营业厅申请宽带。
   nǐ kě yǐ qù zhōng guó diàn xìn yíng yè tīng shēn qǐng kuān dài.

You can go to China Telecom business office for broadband service.

可以提供宽带上网服务的有中国电信、中国移动、中国联通。根据自己的喜好选择任何一家都可以。

China Telecom, China Mobile and China Unicom can provide broadband internet access services. You can choose any one according to your own preferences.

2. 你好，我想办理宽带业务。现在有什么优惠套餐吗？
   nǐ hǎo, wǒ xiǎng bàn lǐ kuān dài yè wù. xiàn zài yǒu shén me yōu huì tào cān ma?

Hello, I'd like to set up broadband service. Are there any special offers now?

不同的宽带品牌会有不同的优惠活动。有的是包年套餐，有的是包月套餐，还有其他类型的优惠。一般来说，如果是长期使用，大部分人都会选择包年套餐，既便宜又省事。

Different broadband brands will have different preferential activities. Some are

· 129 ·

annual packages, some are monthly packages, and there are other types of discounts. Generally speaking, if it is used for a long time, most people will choose the annual package, which is both cheap and easy.

3. 你可以再装一个无线路由器，这样电脑和手机就可以同时使用无线网络了。
nǐ kě yǐ zài zhuāng yí gè wú xiàn lù yóu qì, zhè yàng diàn nǎo hé shǒu jī jiù kě yǐ tóng shí shǐ yòng wú xiàn wǎng luò le.

You can install another wireless router, so that the computer and mobile phone can use the wireless network at the same time.

现在智能手机、平板电脑、笔记本电脑等都已经具备了WiFi功能，大多数人都是办理一条宽带，多个人和多台机器共同使用。这样就必须使用到无线路由器。无线路由器可以在办理宽带的地方购买，也可以在网上商店购买。买回后按照使用说明设置WiFi名称和密码。如果您不是很熟悉路由器的使用规则，还是建议在办理宽带的地方购买，并让安装宽带的师傅一起安装。

Nowadays, smart phones, tablet computers, notebook computers, etc. all have WiFi function, and most people handle a broadband, and many people and machines use it together. Therefore, a wireless router must be used. Wireless routers can be purchased in places where broadband is handled, or in online stores. Set the WiFi name and password according to the instructions after buying it. If you are not familiar with the usage rules of the router, it is recommended to buy it at the place where broadband is handled, and let the broadband installation master install it together.

☞ 实用场景（The Practical Situation）

» 1. 谈论无线网络 Talking about wireless networks

A: 宿舍里有宽带吗？
sù shè lǐ yǒu kuān dài ma?

Do you have broadband in the dormitory?

五、生活娱乐

B：没有，得自己去办。但是学校里有无线网络，用学生证号登陆就行了。

No, you have to do it yourself, but the school has WiFi, so just log in with your student ID number.

A：学校的网络太慢了，我的电脑总是掉线，特别是看电影的时候，一卡一卡的。

The Internet at school is so slow that my computer always drops, especially when I watch movies.

B：你可以去中国电信营业厅申请宽带。

You can go to China Telecom business office to apply for broadband.

A：我周末去看看。

I'm going to visit the China Telecom business office this weekend.

» 2. 在宽带营业厅 In the broadband business hall

A：你好，我想办理宽带业务。现在有什么优惠套餐吗？

Hello, I'd like to set up some broadband service. Are there any special offers now?

B：现在有两种套餐比较划算，一种是50M，720元一年，另一种是100M，960元一年。

At present, there are two kinds of packages that are more cost-effective, one is 50M, 720 *yuan* a year, and the other is 100M, 960 *yuan* a year.

· 131 ·

A：_{wǒ xuǎn 2 0 M de ba}
我 选 ２０Ｍ 的 吧。

I'll take the 20M.

B：_{hǎo de, qǐng bào yí xià nín de diàn huà hào mǎ}
好 的，请 报 一 下 您 的 电 话 号 码。

OK, please tell me your phone number.

3. 设置无线网络 Setting up a wireless network

A：_{kuān dài ān zhuāng hǎo le ma?}
宽 带 安 装 好 了 吗？

Has the broadband been installed?

B：_{ng, gānggāng shī fu lái ān zhuāng hǎo le.}
嗯，刚 刚 师 傅 来 安 装 好 了。

Well, the master has just installed it.

A：_{nǐ kě yǐ zài zhuāng yí gè wú xiàn lù yóu qì, zhè yàng diàn nǎo hé shǒu jī}
你 可 以 再 装 一 个 无 线 路 由 器，这 样 电 脑 和 手 机
_{jiù kě yǐ tóng shí shǐ yòng wú xiàn wǎng luò le.}
就 可 以 同 时 使 用 无 线 网 络 了。

You can install another wireless router, so that the computer and mobile phone can use the wireless network at the same time.

B：_{shì ma? nà wǒ děi mǎi yí gè.}
是 吗？那 我 得 买 一 个。

Isn't it? I'll have to buy one.

核心词汇（Key Words）

序号	词语	拼音	翻译
1	无线网络	wú xiàn wǎng luò	wireless network
2	宽带	kuān dài	broadband

续 表

序号	词语	拼音	翻译
3	上网	shàng wǎng	surf the internet
4	网速	wǎng sù	network speed
5	营业厅	yíng yè tīng	business hall
6	优惠套餐	yōu huì tào cān	discount package
7	包年	bāo nián	yearly package
8	包月	bāo yuè	monthly payment
9	包季	bāo jì	package season

☞ **你知道吗？—— 如何办理宽带？**（Do you know?—— How to Apply for broadband？）

第一种方法：拨打需要装的宽带客服电话。

你如果想安装中国电信宽带，就拨电话10000；你如果想安装中国移动宽带，就拨电话10086；你如果想安装中国联通宽带，就拨电话10010。拨打客服电话，说明你要安装宽带的套餐情况和具体要求，客服人员会派具体的操作人员来家中安装。

第二种方法：到营业厅现场办理。

去宽带营业厅，在柜台上申请办理，说明你要安装宽带的套餐情况和具体要求，后续操作人员去家中安装。

第三种方法：在网上营业厅办理业务。

进入所选宽带品牌的官网，点击宽带业务，进行线上申请和购买。

The first method: dial the broadband customer service telephone that needs to be installed.

If you want to install China Telecom broadband, dial 10000; If you want to install China Mobile broadband, dial 10086; If you want to install China Unicom broadband, dial 10010.Call customer service.Explain to the customer service staff what broadband package and other requirements you need.They will send specific operators to install it at home.

The second method:go to the business hall for on-site installation.

Go to the broadband office and apply at the counter. And then explain to the customer service staff what broadband package and other requirements you need.They will send specific operators to install it at home.

The third method: do business in the online business hall.

Enter the official website of the selected broadband brand, and then click on the broadband business.Apply and purchase online.

去 医 院
Go to the hospital

核心句子 (Kernel Sentence)

1. 你怎么了，看起来很不舒服的样子。
   What's wrong with you? You look sick.

2. 你好，我想挂个号。
   Hello, I'd like to register.

挂号是为了确定次序并便于核查而编号登记。看病之前要先挂号。常规的挂号方式就是在就诊的当天，到医院的挂号窗口，选择挂就诊的科室或者相应的医生的号，在一些医院还可以预先挂后续几天的号。而随着通信工具和互联网的发展，很多医院提供电话预约挂号或者网络预约挂号方式，这种挂号方式也是选择好需要就诊的日期、需要就诊的科室或者医生，然后进行相应的挂号操作。挂号之后，一定要按照预约好的时间、地点

五、生活娱乐

就诊。

——参考有来医生 https://www.youlai.cn/ask/1106BAMkhYa.html

To register by numbers in order to determine order and facilitate checking. You should register before seeing a doctor. The conventional registration method is to select the department to be treated or the corresponding doctor to register in the registration window of the hospital on the day of the visit. Now, some hospitals can also pre-register the number of the following days. With the development of communication tools and the Internet, many hospitals can now make an appointment by telephone or online. This way of registration is to choose the date when they need to see a doctor, and the departments or doctors who need to see a doctor should register accordingly. After registration, you must come to see a doctor at the time and place reserved.

3. 我头疼，好像是发烧了。
   wǒ tóu téng, hǎo xiàng shì fā shāo le.

I have a headache. I think I have a fever.

"头疼"中的"疼"还可以和别的器官进行组合，形式为"A疼"，例如腿疼、肚子疼、眼睛疼、牙齿疼，等等。

The "téng (pain)" which in "tóu téng (headache)" can also be combined with others "A+téng", such as "tuǐ téng (leg pain)", "dù zi téng (stomach pain)", "yǎn jing téng (eye pain)", "yá chǐ téng (tooth pain)",etc.

☞ **实用场景**（The Practical Situation）

» 1. 生病了 Sick

A：你怎么了，看起来很不舒服的样子。
   nǐ zěn me le, kàn qǐ lai hěn bù shū fu de yàng zi.

What's wrong with you? You look sick.

B：我的肚子突然很疼。
   wǒ de dù zi tū rán hěn téng.

I have a sudden pain in my stomach.

· 135 ·

A：wǒ men gǎn kuài qù yī yuàn ba！
我们赶快去医院吧！

Let's go to the hospital at once.

B：hǎo。
好。

OK.

2. 挂号 Register

A：nǐ hǎo，wǒ xiǎng guà gè hào，wài kē。
你好，我想挂个号，外科。

Hello, I'd like to register for surgery.

B：hǎo de，qǐng wèn nín yǒu jiù zhěn kǎ ma？
好的，请问您有就诊卡吗？

OK. Have you got a medical card?

A：méi yǒu。
没有。

No.

B：nà nín xiān tián xiě yì zhāng guà hào biǎo ba。nín de nián líng、xìng bié、zhù zhǐ děng。
那您先填写一张挂号表吧。您的年龄、性别、住址等。

Please fill in a registration card first. Your age, gender, address and so on.

nín yào guà zhuān jiā hào hái shì pǔ tōng hào？
您要挂专家号还是普通号？

Do you want to see a specialist or an ordinary doctor?

3. 检查身体 Checking body

A：nǎr bù shū fu？
哪儿不舒服？

What's your trouble?

B：<ruby>我<rt>wǒ</rt></ruby> <ruby>头疼<rt>tóu téng</rt></ruby>，<ruby>好像<rt>hǎo xiàng</rt></ruby> <ruby>是<rt>shì</rt></ruby> <ruby>发烧<rt>fā shāo</rt></ruby> <ruby>了<rt>le</rt></ruby>。

I have a headache. I think I have a fever.

A：<ruby>除了<rt>chú le</rt></ruby> <ruby>头疼<rt>tóu téng</rt></ruby> <ruby>还有<rt>hái yǒu</rt></ruby> <ruby>什么<rt>shén me</rt></ruby> <ruby>不舒服<rt>bù shū fu</rt></ruby> <ruby>吗<rt>ma</rt></ruby>？<ruby>咳嗽<rt>ké sou</rt></ruby> <ruby>吗<rt>ma</rt></ruby>？

Do you have any discomfort other than a headache? A cough?

B：<ruby>不<rt>bù</rt></ruby> <ruby>咳嗽<rt>ké sou</rt></ruby>，<ruby>就是<rt>jiù shì</rt></ruby> <ruby>头疼<rt>tóu téng</rt></ruby>，<ruby>没有<rt>méi yǒu</rt></ruby> <ruby>力气<rt>lì qi</rt></ruby>。

No cough, just a headache, no energy.

A：<ruby>肺部<rt>fèi bù</rt></ruby> <ruby>听<rt>tīng</rt></ruby> <ruby>起来<rt>qǐ lai</rt></ruby> <ruby>还好<rt>hái hǎo</rt></ruby>，<ruby>先<rt>xiān</rt></ruby> <ruby>去<rt>qù</rt></ruby> <ruby>测<rt>cè</rt></ruby> <ruby>个<rt>gè</rt></ruby> <ruby>体温<rt>tǐ wēn</rt></ruby> <ruby>吧<rt>ba</rt></ruby>，<ruby>然后<rt>rán hòu</rt></ruby> <ruby>去<rt>qù</rt></ruby> <ruby>抽血<rt>chōu xiě</rt></ruby> <ruby>化验<rt>huà yàn</rt></ruby>。<ruby>拿到<rt>ná dào</rt></ruby> <ruby>结果<rt>jié guǒ</rt></ruby> <ruby>再<rt>zài</rt></ruby> <ruby>过来<rt>guò lai</rt></ruby> <ruby>就诊<rt>jiù zhěn</rt></ruby>。

The lungs sounded fine. Let's take your temperature first, and then take a blood test. Come back when you get the results.

B：<ruby>好的<rt>hǎo de</rt></ruby>。

OK.

……

A：<ruby>从<rt>cóng</rt></ruby> <ruby>化验单<rt>huà yàn dān</rt></ruby> <ruby>上<rt>shàng</rt></ruby> <ruby>看<rt>kàn</rt></ruby> <ruby>没<rt>méi</rt></ruby> <ruby>什么<rt>shén me</rt></ruby> <ruby>大<rt>dà</rt></ruby> <ruby>问题<rt>wèn tí</rt></ruby>，<ruby>就是<rt>jiù shì</rt></ruby> <ruby>普通的<rt>pǔ tōng de</rt></ruby> <ruby>流感<rt>liú gǎn</rt></ruby>，<ruby>吃<rt>chī</rt></ruby> <ruby>点<rt>diǎn</rt></ruby> <ruby>药<rt>yào</rt></ruby> <ruby>就<rt>jiù</rt></ruby> <ruby>可以<rt>kě yǐ</rt></ruby> <ruby>了<rt>le</rt></ruby>。<ruby>先<rt>xiān</rt></ruby> <ruby>去<rt>qù</rt></ruby> <ruby>缴费<rt>jiǎo fèi</rt></ruby>，<ruby>然后<rt>rán hòu</rt></ruby> <ruby>去<rt>qù</rt></ruby> <ruby>药房<rt>yào fáng</rt></ruby> <ruby>拿<rt>ná</rt></ruby> <ruby>药<rt>yào</rt></ruby>。<ruby>根据<rt>gēn jù</rt></ruby> <ruby>医嘱<rt>yī zhǔ</rt></ruby> <ruby>每天<rt>měi tiān</rt></ruby> <ruby>吃<rt>chī</rt></ruby> <ruby>药<rt>yào</rt></ruby>。

According to the lab sheets, there's nothing serious. It's just a regular flu. Just take some medicine. First pay the bill, then go to the pharmacy to get the medicine. Take medicine every day as instructed.

B：<ruby>好的<rt>hǎo de</rt></ruby>，<ruby>谢谢<rt>xiè xie</rt></ruby> <ruby>医生<rt>yī shēng</rt></ruby>！

OK, thank you, doctor!

核心词汇（Key Words）

序号	词语	拼音	翻译
1	挂号	guà hào	register
2	医疗指南	yī liáo zhǐ nán	medical guide
3	急诊	jí zhěn	emergency treatment
4	发烧	fā shāo	have a fever
5	咳嗽	ké sou	cough
6	检查	jiǎn chá	check
7	验血	yàn xiě	a blood test
8	手术	shǒu shù	surgery
9	就诊卡	jiù zhěn kǎ	medical card
10	药房	yào fáng	pharmacy
11	检验单	jiǎn yàn dān	inspection sheet

你知道吗？——在中国医院的看病流程（Do you know? Procedures for seeing a doctor in a Chinese hospital）

第一步，填表办理医院的医疗卡。

第二步，排队挂号，例如内科、口腔科等。

第三步，挂号单上有科室的地址，去门诊处排队等待叫号。

第四步，详细真实地说明自己的身体情况，以方便医生快速对症治疗。

第五步，根据医生的要求做相应的检查，例如抽血化验、B超等。

第六步，做完检查拿到结果后，返回门诊室，把检查的结果给医生查看。医生会根据检查结果告诉你病情和治疗方法。

The first step is to fill out the form and apply for the medical card of the hospital.

The second step is to queue up for registration, such as internal medicine and stomatology.

The third step, there is the address of the department on the registration form, go to the outpatient department and wait in line for the call.

The fourth step is to explain one's physical condition in detail and truly, so as to facilitate doctors to treat symptomatic diseases quickly.

The fifth step, according to the doctor's requirements to do the corresponding examination, such as blood test, B-ultrasound, etc.

The sixth step, after getting the examination results, return to the clinic and show the examination results to the doctor. The doctor will tell you the condition and treatment according to the examination results.

微信
WeChat

核心句子 (Kernel Sentence)

1. 我加你微信吧。
   wǒ jiā nǐ wēi xìn ba.

Let me add you on wechat.

"加"在这里的意思是"把本来没有的添上去"。

微信（WeChat）是腾讯公司推出的一个为智能终端提供即时通信服务的免费应用程序。微信通过网络快速发送免费（需消耗少量网络流量）语音短信、视频、图片和文字。此外还有"摇一摇""朋友圈""公众平台""小程序"等服务插件。

——参考360百科"微信"https://baike.so.com/doc/5329667-5564841.html

"jiā" here means "add what you didn't have". WeChat is a free application launched by Tencent to provide instant messaging services for smart terminals. WeChat quickly sends free voice messages, videos, pictures and texts through the network (which consumes a small amount of network traffic). In addition, there are service plug-ins such as "Shake" "Friends Circle" "Public Platform" and "Small Program".

2. 我看到你发的朋友圈啦。
   wǒ kàn dào nǐ fā de péngyouquān la.

I saw your WeChat Moments.

微信用户可以通过朋友圈发表文字、图片和小视频，同时可通过其他软件将文章或者音乐分享到朋友圈。长按发布朋友圈的相机图标，可以进入发布纯文字动态的界面。

图片可以选择拍照或者从相册中选取，一次最多可以分享九张图片。也可以选择拍摄小视频发布分享。用户可以对好友新发的朋友圈进行"评论"或"点赞"。

——参考 360 百科 "微信" https://baike.so.com/doc/5329667-5564841.html

WeChat users can publish texts, pictures and videos through the WeChat Moments, and share articles or music to the WeChat Moments through other software. Long press the camera icon of the publishing WeChat Moments to enter the interface of publishing pure text dynamics.

Pictures can be taken or selected from photo albums, and up to nine pictures can be shared at one time. You can also choose to shoot small videos and share them. Users can "comment" or "like" their friends' new posts.

3. 微信怎么加好友呀？
   wēi xìn zěn me jiā hǎo yǒu ya?

How to add friends on WeChat?

五、生活娱乐

☞ **实用场景**（The Practical Situation）

» 1. 微信 WeChat

A：我加你微信吧，等一会儿把文件发给你。

Let me add you on WeChat and send you the document later.

B：不好意思，我不知道什么是微信。

Sorry, I don't know what WeChat is.

A：微信是一种可以发送语音短信、视频、图片和文字的聊天软件。
可以给好友发信息，也可以多人群聊，很方便的。
现在我们中国人大部分都使用微信。

WeChat is a type of chat software that can send voice messages, videos, pictures and text.

You can send a message to your friends, you also can chat in groups. It is very convenient.

Now most of us Chinese use wechat.

B：好的，那你快教教我吧。我也想试试。

Okay, well, you can teach me. I'd like to try it.

» 2. 朋友圈 WeChat Moment

A：你昨天去看电影了？

nǐ zuó tiān qù kàn diàn yǐng le

Did you go to the movies yesterday?

B：是的呢，你怎么知道啊？

shì de ne, nǐ zěn me zhī dào a

Yeah, how do you know that?

A：我看到你发的朋友圈了。

wǒ kàn dào nǐ fā de péng you quān le

I saw your Wechat Moments.

B：哦，原来如此。要给我点赞哦！

ò, yuán lái rú cǐ. yào gěi wǒ diǎn zàn o

Oh, I see. Give me a thumbs up!

A：知道了！

zhī dào le

I see.

» 3. 加好友 Adding friends

A：微信怎么加好友呀？我看见玛丽的微信里有很多好友。

wēi xìn zěn me jiā hǎo yǒu ya？wǒ kàn jiàn mǎ lì de wēi xìn lǐ yǒu hěn duō hǎo yǒu

How to add friends on WeChat? I see Mary has many friends on wechat.

B：你先打开微信。点这里的"通讯录"，然后点这个"新的朋友""添加朋友"，输入想搜索的微信号码，点击"查找"就可以添加好友了。

nǐ xiān dǎ kāi wēi xìn. diǎn zhè lǐ de "tōng xùn lù", rán hòu diǎn zhè ge "xīn de péng you" "tiān jiā péng you", shū rù xiǎng sōu suǒ de wēi xìn hào mǎ, diǎn jī "chá zhǎo" jiù kě yǐ tiān jiā hǎo yǒu le.

You open WeChat first.Click here "Address book", and then click the "new friend" "Add friends", enter the WeChat number you want to search, click

142

"find" can add friends.

A：嗯，步骤还挺简单的。那如果我不知道对方的微信号码呢，怎么办？

Well, the steps are pretty simple. What should I do if I don't know someone's WeChat number？

B：一般来说，手机号码就是微信号。

Generally speaking, a mobile phone number is a WeChat signal.

A：哦，好的，那我现在把你加为好友吧！

Oh, OK, I'll add you as a friend now!

核心词汇（Key Words）

序号	词语	拼音	翻译
1	聊天	liáo tiān	chat
2	朋友圈	péng yǒu quān	WeChat Moments
3	点赞	diǎn zàn	give a like
4	评论	píng lùn	comments
5	好友	hǎo yǒu	good friend
6	加	jiā	add
7	黑名单	hēi míng dān	blacklist
8	扫一扫	sǎo yi sǎo	scan
9	微信名片	wēi xìn míng piàn	WeChat business card
10	共享位置	gòng xiǎng wèi zhì	shared location
11	语音电话	yǔ yīn diàn huà	voice call
12	视频电话	shì pín diàn huà	video phone
13	微信群	wēi xìn qún	WeChat group

你知道吗？—— 如何申请微信号呢？（Do you know?—— How to apply for a WeChat account？）

微信使用手机号注册，并支持100余个国家的手机号。微信会要求用户设置微信号和昵称。微信号是用户在微信中的唯一识别号，必须大于或等于六位。昵称是微信号的别名，允许多次更改。微信已经逐渐成为办公生活的重要工具，给人们带来了很大的便捷。

——参考百度百科"微信"

https://baike.baidu.com/item/%E5%BE%AE%E4%BF%A1/3905974?fr=aladdin#6_1

那么，如何注册申请微信号呢？

首先你需要下载微信App，然后点击进入微信，点击"注册"。输入昵称、国家、手机号、密码进行注册。一个手机号只支持注册一个微信号。一个微信号只能绑定一个实名信息，绑定后实名信息不能更改，解卡不删除实名绑定关系。

WeChat uses mobile phone numbers to register and supports mobile phone numbers in more than 100 countries. WeChat will ask for micro signals and nicknames. The micro signal is the unique identification number of the user in WeChat, and must be greater than or equal to six digits. Nickname is the alias of micro-signal, which can be changed many times. WeChat has gradually become an important tool in office life, which brings great convenience to people.

So, how to register and apply for micro signal?

First, you need to download the WeChat App, then click to enter WeChat and click "Register". Enter nickname, country, mobile phone number and password to register. Only one micro signal can be registered for one mobile phone number. Only one real-name information can be bound to a micro-signal. After binding, the real-name information cannot be changed. The real-name binding relationship is not deleted when the card is cancelled.

五、生活娱乐

视频网站
Video websites

> 核心句子（Kernel Sentence）

1. <ruby>我<rt>wǒ</rt></ruby><ruby>在<rt>zài</rt></ruby><ruby>优<rt>yōu</rt></ruby><ruby>酷<rt>kù</rt></ruby><ruby>看<rt>kàn</rt></ruby><ruby>电影<rt>diànyǐng</rt></ruby>。

   I watch movies on Youku.

   类似的这种视频网站还有爱奇艺、腾讯视频、芒果TV等。这些视频网站不仅能在电脑上观看，还可以将其App下载到在手机或者iPad上，你可以随时随地观看电视剧或者电影。

   Similar video sites include iQIYI, Tencent Video, Mango TV and so on. These can not only be watched on a computer, but can also be downloaded App on the phone or iPad. You can watch TV shows or movies anytime and anywhere.

2. <ruby>电视剧<rt>diànshìjù</rt></ruby><ruby>就要<rt>jiù yào</rt></ruby><ruby>开始<rt>kāishǐ</rt></ruby><ruby>了<rt>le</rt></ruby>。

   The TV play is about to begin.

   原来电视剧只能在电视上看，现在电视台热播的电视剧，视频网站也会同步更新。并且在视频网站上看，还可以回看、暂停、快进等。多渠道播放模式可以吸引不同年龄层的观众。

   Originally, TV dramas can only be watched on TV. Now, the hot TV series broadcasted by TV stations, video sites will also be updated synchronously. And on the video website, you can also look back, pause, fast forward and so on. Multi-channel broadcasting mode can attract audiences of different ages.

3. <ruby>我<rt>wǒ</rt></ruby><ruby>越来越<rt>yuè lái yuè</rt></ruby><ruby>喜欢<rt>xǐhuan</rt></ruby><ruby>中国<rt>zhōngguó</rt></ruby><ruby>文化<rt>wénhuà</rt></ruby><ruby>了<rt>le</rt></ruby>。

   I like Chinese culture more and more.

实用场景（The Practical Situation）

» 1. 在哪儿看电视剧？ Where did you watch the TV play？

A： nǐ zài kàn shén me?
你在看什么？

What are you looking at?

B： wǒ zài kàn yí gè diàn shì jù, hěn hǎo kàn, ér qiě hái néng xué xí hàn yǔ.
我在看一个电视剧，很好看，而且还能学习汉语。

I'm watching a TV play, the plot is very good, and I can learn to speak Chinese.

A： nǐ zài nǎr kàn de ya?
你在哪儿看的呀？

Where did you watch the TV play？

B： wǒ zài yōu kù kàn de. lǐ miàn hái yǒu hěn duō diàn yǐng、diàn shì jù děng.
我在优酷看的。里面还有很多电影、电视剧等。

I watched it on Youku. There are lots of movies, TV shows and so on.

A： shì miǎn fèi de ma?
是免费的吗？

Is it free?

B： yǒu xiē shì miǎn fèi de, yǒu xiē shì huì yuán cái kě yǐ kàn de. huì yuán kě yǐ àn yuè huò zhě àn nián gòu mǎi.
有些是免费的，有些是会员才可以看的。会员可以按月或者按年购买。

Some are free, and some are for members who can buy on a monthly or yearly basis.

五、生活娱乐

» 2. 看电视剧 Watching TV

A: 玛丽，快来快来，电视剧就要开始了。
mǎ lì, kuài lái kuài lái, diàn shì jù jiù yào kāi shǐ le.

Mary, come on, the TV play is about to start.

B: 好的，我马上来。你先暂停一下。
hǎo de, wǒ mǎ shàng lái. nǐ xiān zàn tíng yí xià.

OK, I'll be right there. Please pause for a moment.

A: 可以开始了吗？
kě yǐ kāi shǐ le ma?

Can we start now?

B: 好了好了。放到第几集了？
hǎo le hǎo le. fàng dào dì jǐ jí le?

All right, all right. What episode is it in?

A: 第六集。还有十集。我们今晚把这个电视剧看完吧？
dì liù jí. hái yǒu shí jí. wǒ men jīn wǎn bǎ zhè ge diàn shì jù kàn wán ba?

Episode 6. Ten more episodes. Shall we finish watching this TV play tonight?

B: 不行，明天还要上课呢。今晚不能熬夜。
bù xíng, míng tiān hái yào shàng kè ne. jīn wǎn bù néng áo yè.

No, we have class tomorrow. I can't stay up late tonight.

» 3. 看视频 Watching video

A: 你在看什么视频？这里的景色好美呀！
nǐ zài kàn shén me shì pín? zhè lǐ de jǐng sè hǎo měi ya!

What video are you watching? The scenery here is so beautiful!

· 147 ·

B：这是李子柒的短视频。她是中国内地美食短视频的创作者。她的视频都是关于中国传统文化的。既有趣又好看。

This is Li Ziqi's short video. She is the creator of short videos of food in the mainland of China. Her videos are all about Chinese traditional culture. It's interesting and beautiful.

A：她的生活真是让人羡慕啊！像生活在仙境里一样。

Her life is really enviable! It's like living in a fairyland.

B：是的，看了她的视频，我越来越喜欢中国文化了。

Yes, I like Chinese culture more and more after watching her video.

A：没错，中国文化真是博大精深，既神秘又美好。

Yes, Chinese culture is profound, mysterious and beautiful.

核心词汇（Key Words）

序号	词语	拼音	翻译
1	电视剧	diàn shì jù	TV series
2	短视频	duǎn shì pín	a short video
3	网红	wǎng hóng	online celebrity
4	播放	bō fàng	play
5	会员	huì yuán	members
6	独播	dú bō	exclusive broadcast
7	原创	yuán chuàng	originality
8	暂停	zàn tíng	suspended
9	快进	kuài jìn	fast forward

五、生活娱乐

续表

序号	词语	拼音	翻译
10	退回	tuì huí	back to

☞ 你知道吗？—— 中国的视频网站（Do you know?—— Chinese video sites）

视频网站是指在完善的技术平台支持下，让互联网用户在线流畅发布、浏览和分享视频作品的网络媒体。中国知名的视频网站有优酷网、爱奇艺、腾讯视频、搜狐视频等。

随着移动终端的普及和网络的提速，短视频逐渐获得各大平台、粉丝和资本的青睐。短视频是指在各种新媒体平台上播放的、适合在移动状态和短时休闲状态下观看的、高频推送的视频内容，几秒到几分钟不等。内容融合了技能分享、幽默搞怪、时尚潮流、社会热点、街头采访、公益教育、广告创意、商业定制等主题。由于内容较短，可以单独成片，也可以成为系列栏目。

——参考百度百科"视频网站"

网址：https://baike.baidu.com/item/%E8%A7%86%E9%A2%91%E7%BD%91%E7%AB%99#8

Video website refers to the network media that allows Internet users to publish, browse and share video works online and smoothly with the support of a perfect technology platform. Well-known video websites in China include Youku, iQIYI, Tencent Video, Sohu Videoand so on.

With the popularity of mobile terminals and the speed-up of the network, short videos have gradually won the favor of major platforms, fans and capital. Short video refers to the video content played on various new media platforms, which is suitable for watching in mobile state and short-term leisure state and pushed at high frequency. The duration varies from seconds to minutes. The content combines skills sharing, humor and whimsy, fashion trends, social hotspots, street interviews, public welfare education, advertising creativity, business customization and other topics. Because the content is short, it can be made into a single piece or a series of columns.

过春节
Celebrating the Spring Festival

核心句子（Kernel Sentence）

1. 明天是大年三十，你来我家包饺子吧？

Tomorrow is Chinese New Year's eve, why don't you come to my house to make dumplings?

北方年夜饭有吃饺子的传统，吃饺子是表达人们祈福、求吉愿望的特有方式。另外，饺子形状像元宝，包饺子意味着包住福运，吃饺子象征生活富裕。与北方不同，南方的年夜饭通常有火锅和鱼。火锅沸煮，热气腾腾，红红火火；"鱼"和"余"谐音，象征"吉庆有余"，也喻示着生活幸福，"年年有余"。

——参考360百科"饺子"https://baike.so.com/doc/5390775-5627426.html

There is a tradition of eating dumplings at the New Year's Eve dinner in northern China. Eating dumplings is a special way to express people's wishes for good luck. In addition, dumplings are shaped like ingot. Making dumplings means wrapping up good luck and eating dumplings symbolizes prosperity. Unlike the North, the New Year's Eve dinner in the south usually has hot pot and fish. Hot pot boiling, steaming hot, booming; "yú(fish)" sounds like "yú(surplus)", it symbolizes "more than auspicious", it also indicates a happy life, "more than every year".

2. 我们送他一个中国结挂件吧。

Let's give him a Chinese knot.

中国结是一种手工编织工艺品，代表着团结、幸福、平安，特别是在

五、生活娱乐

民间，它精致的做工深受大众的喜爱。

——参考360百科"中国结"https://baike.so.com/doc/1207058-1276830.html

Chinese knot is a hand-woven handicraft, which represents unity, happiness and peace, especially in the folk, and its exquisite workmanship is deeply loved by the public.

3. liú lǎo shī, guò nián hǎo! gěi nín bài nián la!
刘老师，过年好！给您拜年啦！

Miss Liu! Happy New Year to you! Best wishes to you!

拜年是中国民间的传统习俗，是人们辞旧迎新、相互表达美好祝愿的一种方式。古时"拜年"的含义是为长者拜贺新年。随着时代的发展，拜年的习俗亦不断增添新的内容和形式。除了沿袭以往的拜年方式外，又兴起了电话拜年、短信拜年、网络拜年等。

——参考360百科"拜年"https://baike.so.com/doc/6198977-6412239.html

New Year greeting is a traditional custom in China. It is a way for people to bid farewell to the old year and usher in the New Year and express good wishes to each other.In ancient times, the meaning of "New Year greeting" is to pay a New Year's visit to the elderly.With the development of the times, the custom of New Year also constantly add new content and form.In addition to follow the previous way, and the rise of the telephone, SMS, network, etc.

☞ 实用场景（The Practical Situation）

» 1. 包饺子 Making dumplings

A：mǎ lì, nǐ shì dì yī cì zài zhōng guó guò nián ba?
玛丽，你是第一次在中国过年吧？

Mary, is it your first time to spend the Spring Festival in China?

B：shì de, dì yī cì ne.
是的，第一次呢。

Yes, the first time.

A：míngtiān shì dà nián sān shí, nǐ lái wǒ jiā bāo jiǎo zi ba?
明天是大年三十，你来我家包饺子吧？

Tomorrow is Chinese New Year's eve, why don't you come to my house to make dumplings?

B：hǎo ya, wǒ hái méi yǒu bāo guo jiǎo zi ne。wǒ míng tiān yí dìng guò qu。xiè xie nǐ!
好呀，我还没有包过饺子呢。我明天一定过去。谢谢你！

Sure. I've never made dumplings before. I'll be there tomorrow. Thank you very much.

» 2. 送礼物 Sending a Gift

A：míng tiān qù wáng gāng jiā chī jiǎo zi, nǐ shuō, wǒ men mǎi shén me yàng de lǐ wù sòng gěi tā men hé shì ne?
明天去王刚家吃饺子，你说，我们买什么样的礼物送给他们合适呢？

Tomorrow we are going to eat dumplings at Wang Gang's. What kind of gift do you think we should buy for them?

B：wǒ jué de zhè ge tǐng hǎo de。
我觉得这个挺好的。

I think this is good.

A：bù hǎo bù hǎo。dà guò nián de sòng yì běn shū dāng lǐ wù bú tài hé shì ba。
不好不好。大过年的送一本书当礼物不太合适吧。

Not good. A book is not an appropriate gift for Chinese New Year.

B：nà sòng yí ge zhōng guó jié guà jiàn ne? hóng sè tǐng hǎo kàn de, yù yì lái nián néng gòu hóng hóng huǒ huǒ。
那送一个中国结挂件呢？红色挺好看的，寓意来年能够红红火火。

How about a Chinese knot pendant? Red is very beautiful, meaning that the coming year will be prosperous.

A：这个好！听说中国人过春节的时候都要穿红色的衣服，贴红色的福字，我们送一对红色的中国结正好！

This is good! It is said that Chinese people wear red clothes and stick the red character "fú" on the Spring Festival. It is good for us to send a pair of red Chinese knots!

B：行，那就买吧。

OK, I'll take it.

3. 拜年 Pay a New Year call

A：刘老师，过年好！给您拜年啦！

Miss Liu! Happy New Year to you! Best wishes to you!

B：谢谢！也祝王老师您牛年大吉啊！越活越年轻！

Thank you very much! I also wish Mr. Wang a prosperous Year of the Ox! The younger you live!

A：来这边坐，吃点糕点，喝点茶。

Here, sit down and have some cake and tea.

B：好的，谢谢！

OK, thank you.

核心词汇 (Key Words)

序号	词语	拼音	翻译
1	春节	chūn jié	Spring Festival
2	饺子	jiǎo zi	dumplings
3	火锅	huǒ guō	hot pot
4	年糕	nián gāo	rice cake
5	拜年	bài nián	Happy New Year
6	窗花	chuāng huā	paper-cut for window decoration
7	对联	duì lián	couplets
8	福字	fú zì	character "fú"
9	元宵	yuán xiāo	glutinous rice ball for Lantern Festival
10	春卷	chūn juǎn	spring rolls
11	春晚	chūn wǎn	Spring Festival Gala
12	爆竹	bào zhú	firecracker
13	守岁	shǒu suì	stay up late or all night on New Year's Eve

你知道吗？—— 春节 (Do you know?—— Spring Festival)

春节，即农历新年，俗称过年，一般从腊月二十三的祭灶到正月十五，也有的从腊月初八开始，一直过到正月底，其中以除夕和大年初一为高潮。春节时间延续长、地域跨度广，节日活动丰富，是我国最重要、最隆重，也是历史最悠久、最热闹的传统节日。中国人民过春节已有4000多年的历史。在漫长悠久的历史岁月中，春节从萌芽到定型，不断发展，形成独具中华民族特色、丰富多彩的习俗。春节期间的活动以祭祖敬老、感恩祈福、阖家团聚、除旧布新、迎禧接福、祈求丰年为主要内容。春联、年画、爆竹、压岁钱、花灯是春节最具有代表性的五种吉祥物。

Spring Festival, the Lunar New Year, is commonly known as Chinese New Year. It generally starts from the kitchen sacrifice on the 23rd day of the twelfth lunar month to the 15th day of the first lunar month, and also starts from the 8th day of the twelfth lunar month to the end of the month, with New Year's Eve and New Year's Day as the climax. Spring Festival is the most important and grand traditional festival in China, with its long duration, wide geographical span and rich festival activities. Chinese people have celebrated Spring Festival for more than 4000 years. In the long and long history, Spring Festival has developed continuously from germination to finalization, forming a unique and colorful custom with Chinese national characteristics. During the Spring Festival, the activities mainly focus on worshipping the ancestors and the elderly, giving thanks and praying for blessings, reuniting the whole family, removing the old and making new clothes, welcoming the jubilee and receiving blessings, and praying for a good year. Spring Festival couplets, New Year pictures, firecrackers, lucky money and lanterns are the five most representative mascots of Spring Festival.

附 录
Appendix

核心句汇总 (Core sentence summary)

1. qǐng wèn, nín zhī dào jiào xué lóu zěn me zǒu ma?
   请问，您知道教学楼怎么走吗？
   Excuse me, do you know how to get to the teaching building?

2. nín kě yǐ bāng wǒ huà yì zhāng dì tú ma?
   您可以帮我画一张地图吗？
   Can you draw a map for me?

3. yán zhe zhè tiáo lù yì zhí wǎng qián zǒu, dào le dì èr gè lù kǒu wǎng yòu guǎi.
   沿着这条路一直往前走，到了第二个路口往右拐。
   Go straight along this road and turn right at the second crossing.

4. zhè shì wǒ men de kè biǎo.
   这是我们的课表。
   This is our class schedule.

5. nǐ měi tiān yǒu duō shǎo jié kè?
   你每天有多少节课？
   How many classes do you have every day?

6. wǒ men bú yào chí dào le.
   我们不要迟到了。
   Don't be late.

7. 你一共有多少门汉语课？
   nǐ yí gòng yǒu duō shǎo mén hàn yǔ kè?

   How many Chinese courses do you have altogether?

8. 张老师对我们非常严格。
   zhāng lǎo shī duì wǒ men fēi cháng yán gé.

   Mr. Zhang is very strict with us.

9. 每天下课都布置作业。
   měi tiān xià kè dōu bù zhì zuò yè.

   Homework is assigned every day after class.

10. 请问你（您）叫什么名字？
    qǐng wèn nǐ (nín) jiào shén me míng zi?

    What's your name, please?

11. 我是韩国人。
    wǒ shì hán guó rén.

    I'm Korean.

12. 你（您）好。
    nǐ (nín) hǎo.

    How do you do? /Hello.

13. 请问，听力课什么时候考试？
    qǐng wèn, tīng lì kè shén me shí hou kǎo shì?

    Excuse me, when is the listening test?

14. 期末考试是闭卷考试，请大家遵守考试纪律。
    qī mò kǎo shì shì bì juàn kǎo shì, qǐng dà jiā zūn shǒu kǎo shì jì lǜ.

    The final exam is a closed-book exam. Please observe the discipline of the examination.

15. 期末考试考得怎么样？
    qī mò kǎo shì kǎo de zěn me yàng?

    How is your final exam?

16. 中秋节就要到了，我们要放三天假。
zhōng qiū jié jiù yào dào le, wǒ men yào fàng sān tiān jià.

The Mid-Autumn Festival is coming, we will have a three-day holiday.

17. 除了暑假、寒假，还有其他很多假期。
chú le shǔ jià, hán jià, hái yǒu qí tā hěn duō jià qī.

There are many other holidays besides summer vacation and winter vacation.

18. 我们什么时候放寒假？
wǒ men shén me shí hou fàng hán jià?

When is the winter holiday?

19. 你去哪儿吃饭？
nǐ qù nǎr chī fàn?

Where do you want to eat?

20. 我们去万达吃饭怎么样？
wǒ men qù wàn dá chī fàn zěn me yàng?

Shall we go to Wanda for dinner?

21. 你想吃什么？
nǐ xiǎng chī shén me?

What would you want to eat?

22. 我要一个包子和一杯豆浆。
wǒ yào yí gè bāo zi hé yì bēi dòu jiāng.

I want a steamed stuffed bun and a cup of soybean milk.

23. 请把餐盘和垃圾带走，放到出口的餐盘回收处。
qǐng bǎ cān pán hé lā jī dài zǒu, fàng dào chū kǒu de cān pán huí shōu chù.

Please take your plates and garbage away and put them in the tray recycling area at the exit.

24. wǒ yào dǎ bāo .
    我要打包。

    I want to pack the food.

    I need a doggy bag.

25. qǐng wèn nín xiàn zài yào diǎn cān ma ?
    请问您现在要点餐吗？

    May I take your order now?

26. jīn tiān yǒu shén me tè jià cài ma ?
    今天有什么特价菜吗？

    Do you have any special today?

27. diǎn cān qǐng sǎo mǎ .
    点餐请扫码。

    Please scan the code to order.

28. fú wù yuán , mǎi dān .
    服务员，买单。

    Excuse me, bill please.

29. jīn tiān wǒ qǐng kè .
    今天我请客。

    It's on me today.

    It's my treat today.

30. nín zěn me fù kuǎn ? shì yòng wēi xìn 、 zhī fù bǎo hái shì xiàn jīn ?
    您怎么付款？是用微信、支付宝还是现金？

    How would you like to pay? WeChat, Alipay or cash？

31. bāng wǒ ná yí gè dǎ bāo hé .
    帮我拿一个打包盒。

    Get me a to-go box.

32. shì zài zhèr chī hái shì dǎ bāo dài zǒu?
    是在这儿吃还是打包带走？
    Is that for here or to go?

33. zhè ge dǎ bāo hé bù néng zhí jiē fàng wēi bō lú.
    这个打包盒不能直接放微波炉。
    You can't put this to-go box in the microwave oven.

34. yào bù wǒ men diǎn wài mài chī ba?
    要不我们点外卖吃吧？
    Why don't we order some take-away food?

35. nín diǎn de wài mài dào le, qǐng xià lóu lái qǔ yí xià.
    您点的外卖到了，请下楼来取一下。
    Your take-away food has arrived. Please come down to get it.

36. wǒ gāng gāng diǎn le yí fèn zhá jī, qǐng wèn shén me shí hou kě yǐ sòng dào?
    我刚刚点了一份炸鸡，请问什么时候可以送到？
    I just ordered some fried chicken. When will it be delivered?

37. niú ròu zěn me mài?
    牛肉怎么卖？
    How much is the beef?

38. nǐ xiǎng mǎi diǎnr shén me?
    你想买点儿什么？
    What do you want to buy?

39. kě yǐ pián yi yì diǎnr ma?
    可以便宜一点儿吗？
    Can you make it a little cheaper?

40. 您好，这里有购物车和购物篮，您可以自取。

Hello, here are shopping carts and baskets. You can pick them up by yourself.

41. 在哪儿称重？

Where can I weigh it?

42. 一共消费87元，请问您有会员卡吗？

The total cost is 87 *yuan*. Do you have a membership card?

43. 想去哪儿逛？

Where do you want to go?

44. 这条连衣裙看起来不错，我能试试吗？

This dress looks nice. Can I try it on?

45. 原价400元，现在打八折，320元。

The original price is 400 *yuan*, and now it's 20 percent off, 320 *yuan*.

46. 在网上买东西既方便又便宜。

It's convenient and cheap to buy things online.

47. 请问这件连衣裙有货吗？

Is this dress in stock?

48. 亲，喜欢可以下单试试呢。

Dear, if you like, you can have a try.

· 161 ·

49. 您是想退还是想欢呢？
nín shì xiǎng tuì huán shì xiǎng huàn ne?

Do you want to return it or exchange it?

50. 好的，您申请退款，按照给的地址寄回来就行了。邮费自付哦。
hǎo de, nín shēn qǐng tuì kuǎn, àn zhào gěi de dì zhǐ jì huí lai jiù xíng le. yóu fèi zì fù o.

OK, you apply for a refund and send it back to the address given. Postage pays.

51. 我买的连衣裙码数发错了。
wǒ mǎi de lián yī qún mǎ shù fā cuò le.

The dress I bought was given the wrong size.

52. 我要寄一个快递。
wǒ yào jì yí gè kuài dì.

I want to send an express.

53. 请您先扫一下这里的二维码，填写收货人的地址和电话，还有寄货人的电话。
qǐng nín xiān sǎo yí xià zhè lǐ de èr wéi mǎ, tián xiě shōu huò rén de dì zhǐ hé diàn huà, hái yǒu jì huò rén de diàn huà.

Please scan the QR code here first. Fill in the address and telephone number of the consignee, and the phone number of the shipper.

54. 请问您需要办理加急业务吗？
qǐng wèn nín xū yào bàn lǐ jiā jí yè wù ma?

Do you need any urgent service?

55. 我去万达应该坐几路公交车？
wǒ qù wàn dá yīng gāi zuò jǐ lù gōng jiāo chē?

Which bus should I take to go to Wanda?

56. 6路车从学校到万达要坐几站？
6 lù chē cóng xué xiào dào wàn dá yào zuò jǐ zhàn?

How many stops does the No.6 bus take from school to Wanda?

附 录

57. nǐ kě yǐ zhǎo qí tā chéng kè huànqián, wǒ men bù zhǎolíng.
    你可以找其他乘客换钱，我们不找零。
    You can change money with other passengers. We don't give change.

58. nín yào qù nǎr?
    您要去哪儿？
    Where are you going?

59. má fan nín kuài yì diǎnr, wǒ yào gǎn huǒ chē.
    麻烦您快一点儿，我要赶火车。
    Please hurry up, I have a train to catch.

60. nǐ yào zài nǎr xià chē?
    你要在哪儿下车？
    Where do you want to get off?

61. zuì jìn de dì tiě zhàn zài nǎr?
    最近的地铁站在哪儿？
    Where is the nearest subway station?

62. nǐ kě yǐ zài shòupiàochuāng kǒu huò zhě zì dòngshòupiào jī shàngmǎi piào.
    你可以在售票窗口或者自动售票机上买票。
    You can buy tickets at the ticket window or the machine.

63. qǐngwèn wǒ yào qù shì jì gōngyuányīng gāi zuò jǐ hào xiàn?
    请问我要去世纪公园应该坐几号线？
    Could you tell me which line I should take to go to Century Park?

64. mǎi yì zhāngmíngtiān qù shànghǎi de piào.
    买一张明天去上海的票。
    A ticket to Shanghai for tomorrow.

65. qù gāo tiě zhàn huò zhě zài shǒu jī App shàngmǎi.
    去高铁站或者在手机 App 上买。
    Go to a high-speed train station or buy it on a mobile App.

· 163 ·

66. 请问餐车在几号车厢？
    qǐng wèn cān chē zài jǐ hào chē xiāng?
    Which compartment is the dining car, please?

67. 我想现在预订往返机票，比较划算。
    wǒ xiǎng xiàn zài yù dìng wǎng fǎn jī piào, bǐ jiào huá suàn.
    I want to book a round-trip ticket now. It's cheaper.

68. 我想订一张2月13号去哈尔滨的机票。
    wǒ xiǎng dìng yì zhāng 2 yuè 13 hào qù hā ěr bīn de jī piào.
    I want to book a ticket to Harbin on February 13th.

69. 请问您要喝点什么？
    qǐng wèn nín yào hē diǎn shén me?
    What would you like to drink?

70. 我想预订一个标间。
    wǒ xiǎng yù dìng yí gè biāo jiān.
    I'd like to reserve a standard room.

71. 等一会儿订房信息会发送到您手机上，请注意查收。
    děng yí huìr dìng fáng xìn xī huì fā sòng dào nín shǒu jī shàng, qǐng zhù yì chá shōu.
    The reservation information will be sent to your phone later, please check it.

72. 请问你们有没有接机服务？
    qǐng wèn nǐ men yǒu méi yǒu jiē jī fú wù?
    Do you have airport pick-up service?

73. 您好，我要办理入住。
    nín hǎo, wǒ yào bàn lǐ rù zhù.
    Hello, I'd like to check in, please.

74. 这是您的房卡和早餐券。
zhè shì nín de fáng kǎ hé zǎo cān quàn.

Here is your room card and breakfast coupon.

75. 服务员，我房间的马桶有问题，你可以过来看看吗？
fú wù yuán, wǒ fáng jiān de mǎ tǒng yǒu wèn tí, nǐ kě yǐ guò lai kàn kan ma?

Waiter, there is something wrong with the toilet in my room. Can you come and have a look?

76. 你喜欢什么类型的电影？
nǐ xǐ huan shén me lèi xíng de diàn yǐng?

What kind of movies do you like?

77. 我昨天看了一部喜剧片，可好看了！
wǒ zuó tiān kàn le yí bù xǐ jù piàn, kě hǎo kàn le!

I watched a comedy yesterday, it was so good!

78. 我们去哪儿看电影啊？
wǒ men qù nǎr kàn diàn yǐng a?

Where shall we go to see the movie?

79. 你好，我要换钱。
nǐ hǎo, wǒ yào huàn qián.

Hello, I'd like to change some money.

80. 我想开通一个银行账户。
wǒ xiǎng kāi tōng yí gè yín háng zhàng hù.

I'd like to open a bank account.

81. 赶快拨打银行客服电话临时挂失。
gǎn kuài bō dǎ yín háng kè fú diàn huà lín shí guà shī.

Call the bank customer service phone and report the loss temporarily.

82. 可以在网上租，有专门的租房网站，也可以去找房产中介。

You can rent online, there are special rental websites, or you can go to a real estate agent.

83. 我想租一套一室一厅的公寓，要有厨房和卫生间。

I want to rent a one-bedroom apartment with a kitchen and a bathroom.

84. 一个月1800，押一付一，半年起租。

The rent is 1800 *yuan* a month, pay one month's rent and one month's deposit. Rental time at least six months.

85. 你可以去中国电信营业厅申请宽带。

You can go to China Telecom business office for broadband service.

86. 你好，我想办理宽带业务。现在有什么优惠套餐吗？

Hello, I'd like to set up broadband service. Are there any special offers now?

87. 你可以再装一个无线路由器，这样电脑和手机就可以同时使用无线网络了。

You can install another wireless router, so that the computer and mobile phone can use the wireless network at the same time.

88. 你怎么了，看起来很不舒服的样子。

What's wrong with you? You look sick.

89. 你好，我想挂个号。
nǐ hǎo, wǒ xiǎng guà gè hào.
Hello, I'd like to register.

90. 我头疼，好像是发烧了。
wǒ tóu téng, hǎo xiàng shì fā shāo le.
I have a headache. I think I have a fever.

91. 我加你微信吧。
wǒ jiā nǐ wēi xìn ba.
Let me add you on WeChat.

92. 我看到你发的朋友圈啦。
wǒ kàn dào nǐ fā de péng you quān la.
I saw your WeChat Moments.

93. 微信怎么加好友呀？
wēi xìn zěn me jiā hǎo yǒu ya?
How to add friends on WeChat?

94. 我在优酷看电影。
wǒ zài yōu kù kàn diàn yǐng.
I watch movies on Youku.

95. 电视剧就要开始了。
diàn shì jù jiù yào kāi shǐ le.
The TV play is about to begin.

96. 我越来越喜欢中国文化了。
wǒ yuè lái yuè xǐ huan zhōng guó wén huà le.
I like Chinese culture more and more.

97. 明天大年三十，你来我家包饺子吧？
míng tiān dà nián sān shí, nǐ lái wǒ jiā bāo jiǎo zi ba?
Tomorrow is Chinese New Year's eve, why don't you come to my house to make dumplings?

98. wǒ men sòng tā yí gè zhōng guó jié guà jiàn ba．
    我们送他一个中国结挂件吧。
    Let's give him a Chinese knot.

99. liú lǎo shī， guò nián hǎo！ gěi nín bài nián la！
    刘老师，过年好！给您拜年啦！
    Miss Liu! Happy New Year to you! Best wishes to you！

核心词汇总（Core word summary）

序号	词语	拼音	翻译	课
1	2号线	2 hào xiàn	line 2	21
2	安排	ān pái	to arrange	2
3	安全带	ān quán dài	seat belt	20
4	白菜	bái cài	Chinese cabbage	13
5	拜年	bài nián	Happy New Year	33
6	办公室	bàn gōng shì	office	1
7	包季	bāo jì	package season	29
8	包年	bāo nián	yearly package	29
9	包邮	bāo yóu	exemption from postage	17
10	包月	bāo yuè	monthly payment	29
11	包子	bāo zi	steamed stuffed bun	7
12	便宜	pián yi	cheap	13
13	标间	biāo jiān	standard room	24
14	饼	bǐng	pancake	8
15	播放	bō fàng	play	32
16	不太好	bú tài hǎo	not so well	5
17	菜单	cài dān	menu	9

续表

序号	词语	拼音	翻译	课
18	餐车	cān chē	dining car	22
19	餐盘	cān pán	plate	8
20	餐厅	cān tīng	dining room	28
21	场次	chǎng cì	session	26
22	超市	chāo shì	supermarket	4
23	炒菜	chǎo cài	stir-fry dish	7
24	炒面	chǎo miàn	fried noodles	7
25	衬衣	chèn yī	shirt	15
26	称重	chēng zhòng	to weigh	14
27	乘客	chéng kè	passengers	19
28	吃饭	chī fàn	have a meal	7
29	迟到	chí dào	late	2
30	出租车	chū zū chē	taxi	20
31	厨房	chú fáng	kitchen	28
32	窗花	chuāng huā	paper-cut for window decoration	33
33	春节	chūn jié	Spring Festival	6
34	春卷	chūn juǎn	spring rolls	33
35	春晚	chūn wǎn	Spring Festival Gala	33
36	春运	chūn yùn	Spring Festival travel season	23
37	打包	dǎ bāo	to pack	11
38	打包盒	dǎ bāo hé	to-go box	11
39	打折	dǎ zhé	at a discount	14
40	大床房	dà chuáng fáng	big bed room	24
41	大门	dà mén	gate	1

续 表

序 号	词 语	拼 音	翻 译	课
42	带走	dài zǒu	to take away	11
43	单人间	dān rén jiān	single room	24
44	地铁票	dì tiě piào	subway ticket	21
45	地铁站	dì tiě zhàn	subway station	21
46	地图	dì tú	map	1
47	地址	dì zhǐ	address	12
48	灯	dēng	lamp	25
49	点餐	diǎn cān	to order	9
50	点赞	diǎn zàn	give a like	31
51	电费	diàn fèi	power rate	28
52	电视	diàn shì	TV	25
53	电视剧	diàn shì jù	TV series	32
54	电影	diàn yǐng	film	26
55	电影票	diàn yǐng piào	movie ticket	26
56	电影院	diàn yǐng yuàn	cinema	26
57	订单号	dìng dān hào	order number	17
58	东坡肉	dōng pō ròu	Dongpo pork	9
59	豆浆	dòu jiāng	soybean milk	7
60	独播	dú bō	exclusive broadcast	32
61	端午节	duān wǔ jié	Dragon Boat Festival	6
62	短视频	duǎn shì pín	a short video	32
63	对联	duì lián	couplets	33
64	二等座	èr děng zuò	second class	22
65	发货	fā huò	to deliver goods	16

续表

序号	词语	拼音	翻译	课
66	发烧	fā shāo	have a fever	30
67	发音	fā yīn	pronunciation	3
68	方便	fāng biàn	convenient	16
69	房卡	fáng kǎ	room card	25
70	房租	fáng zū	rent	28
71	服务员	fú wù yuán	waiter	10
72	福字	fú zì	character "fú"	33
73	付款	fù kuǎn	payment	10
74	复习	fù xí	to review	5
75	高铁站	gāo tiě zhàn	high-speed railway station	20
76	公交车	gōng jiāo chē	bus	19
77	公交卡	gōng jiāo kǎ	bus card	19
78	公交站	gōng jiāo zhàn	bus station	19
79	公寓	gōng yù	apartment	28
80	共享位置	gòng xiǎng wèi zhì	shared location	31
81	购物车	gòu wù chē	shopping cart	14
82	购物篮	gòu wù lán	shopping basket	14
83	挂号	guà hào	register	30
84	挂失	guà shī	report the loss	27
85	逛街	guàng jiē	to go shopping	15
86	国家	guó jiā	country	4
87	国庆节	guó qìng jié	National Day	6
88	咳嗽	ké sou	cough	30
89	还可以	hái kě yǐ	not bad	5

续 表

序 号	词 语	拼 音	翻 译	课
90	韩国	hán guó	Republic of Korea	4
91	寒假	hán jià	winter vacation	6
92	好友	hǎo yǒu	good friend	31
93	合适	hé shì	appropriate	15
94	合同	hé tóng	contract	28
95	合租	hé zū	flat sharing	28
96	贺岁片	hè suì piàn	Chinese New Year film	26
97	黑名单	hēi míng dān	blacklist	31
98	护照	hù zhào	passport	27
99	划算	huá suàn	cost-effective	23
100	换乘	huàn chéng	to transfer	21
101	换货	huàn huò	to exchange goods	17
102	换钱	huàn qián	change money	27
103	回收处	huí shōu chù	recycling place	8
104	会员	huì yuán	members	32
105	会员卡	huì yuán kǎ	membership card	14
106	火车票	huǒ chē piào	train ticket	22
107	火锅	huǒ guō	hot pot	33
108	机票	jī piào	the air ticket	23
109	鸡肉	jī ròu	chicken	13
110	急诊	jí zhěn	emergency treatment	30
111	纪律	jì lǜ	discipline	5
112	忌口	jì kǒu	to avoid certain food	9
113	寄	jì	send	18

续表

序 号	词 语	拼 音	翻 译	课
114	寄件人	jì jiàn rén	sender	18
115	加	jiā	add	31
116	加急	jiā jí	urgent	18
117	加热	jiā rè	to heat	11
118	价钱	jià qián	price	8
119	检查	jiǎn chá	check	30
120	检验单	jiǎn yàn dān	inspection sheet	30
121	饺子	jiǎo zi	dumplings	7/33
122	叫	jiào	to call	4
123	叫醒服务	jiào xǐng fú wù	wake-up service	25
124	节	jié	section	2
125	节日	jié rì	holiday	6
126	斤	jīn	catty/jin(a unit of weight =0.5 kilograms)	13
127	经济舱	jīng jì cāng	economy class	23
128	纠正	jiū zhèng	to correct	3
129	就诊卡	jiù zhěn kǎ	medical card	30
130	看起来	kàn qǐ lai	to look	15
131	考试	kǎo shì	test	5
132	客服	kè fú	customer service	16
133	客厅	kè tīng	sitting room	28
134	空调	kōng tiáo	air conditioning	25
135	口语课	kǒu yǔ kè	oral course	3
136	苦	kǔ	bitter	9
137	裤子	kù zi	trousers	15

续 表

序 号	词 语	拼 音	翻 译	课
138	快递	kuài dì	express delivery	18
139	快递单号	kuài dì dān hào	courier number	18
140	快递费	kuài dì fèi	express fee	18
141	快递员	kuài dì yuán	courier	18
142	快递站	kuài dì zhàn	express station	18
143	快进	kuài jìn	fast forward	32
144	宽带	kuān dài	broadband	29
145	垃圾	lā jī	garbage	8
145	辣	là	spicy	9
146	浪费	làng fèi	to waste	11
147	离	lí	from	1
148	梨子	lí zi	pear	13
149	聊天	liáo tiān	chat	31
150	零钱	líng qián	change	19
151	零食	líng shí	snacks	14
152	留学生	liú xué shēng	international students	1
153	路口	lù kǒu	crossroads	1
154	萝卜	luó bo	radish	13
155	麻婆豆腐	má pó dòu fu	Mapo Tofu	9
156	马上	mǎ shàng	immediately	2
157	马桶	mǎ tǒng	toilet	25
158	买单	mǎi dān	to pay the bill	10
159	馒头	mán tou	steamed the bread	8
160	忙	máng	busy	3

续 表

序 号	词 语	拼 音	翻 译	课
161	美国	měi guó	United States	4
162	美元	měi yuán	dollar	27
163	门	mén	measure word	3
164	米饭	mǐ fàn	rice	7
165	密码	mì mǎ	password	27
166	名字	míng zi	name	4
167	明天	míng tiān	tomorrow	22
168	难	nán	difficult	5
169	你好	nǐ hǎo	hello	4
170	年糕	nián gāo	rice cake	33
171	牛肉	niú ròu	beef	13
172	爆竹	bào zhú	firecracker	33
173	朋友圈	péng yǒu quān	WeChat Moments	31
174	比萨	bǐ sà	pizza	12
175	评论	píng lùn	comments	31
176	苹果	píng guǒ	apple	13
177	起始票	qǐ shǐ piào	starting ticket	21
178	前台电话	qián tái diàn huà	front desk telephone	25
179	亲	qīn	honey	16
180	清明节	qīng míng jié	Qingming Festival	6
181	请客	qǐng kè	to entertain guests	10
182	取	qǔ	take	12
183	取件码	qǔ jiàn mǎ	pick-up code	18
184	取消	qǔ xiāo	cancel	24

续 表

序 号	词 语	拼 音	翻 译	课
185	去哪儿	qù nǎr	Where to go?	26
186	裙子	qún zi	skirt	15
187	热干面	rè gān miàn	hot-and-dry noodles	7
188	人民币	rén mín bì	RMB	27
189	日本	rì běn	Japan	4
190	日元	rì yuán	Japanese yen	27
191	入口	rù kǒu	entrance	21
192	入住	rù zhù	be opened for occupancy	25
193	扫码	sǎo mǎ	to scan the code	10
194	扫一扫	sǎo yi sǎo	scan	31
195	商场	shāng chǎng	mall	15
196	商品	shāng pǐn	goods	14
197	上网	shàng wǎng	surf the Internet	16/29
198	上午	shàng wǔ	morning	2
199	上映	shàng yìng	release/show	26
200	烧水壶	shāo shuǐ hú	kettle	25
201	时间	shí jiān	time	2
202	时刻表	shí kè biǎo	timetable	19
203	试穿	shì chuān	to try it on	15
204	试衣间	shì yī jiān	fitting room	15
205	视频电话	shì pín diàn huà	video phone	31
206	收货	shōu huò	to receive goods	16
207	收件人	shōu jiàn rén	recipient	18
208	手术	shǒu shù	surgery	30

续 表

序 号	词 语	拼 音	翻 译	课
209	守岁	shǒu suì	stay up late or all night on New Year's Eve	33
210	售货员	shòu huò yuán	salesman	14
211	售票窗口	shòu piào chuāng kǒu	ticket window	21
212	暑假	shǔ jià	summer vacation	6
213	刷卡	shuā kǎ	to swipe card	8
214	水费	shuǐ fèi	water rate	28
215	水龙头	shuǐ lóng tóu	water tap	25
216	宿舍	sù shè	dormitory	1
217	酸	suān	sour	9
218	酸菜鱼	suān cài yú	fish with sauerkraut	9
219	汤圆	tāng yuán	sweet soup balls	6
220	糖醋里脊	táng cù lǐ ji	sweet and sour fillet of pork	7
221	套房	tào fáng	suite	24
222	特价菜	tè jià cài	special	9
223	甜	tián	sweet	9
224	条形码	tiáo xíng mǎ	bar code	14
225	听力课	tīng lì kè	listening course	3
226	头等舱	tóu děng cāng	first class	23
227	投币	tóu bì	to coin	19
228	图书馆	tú shū guǎn	library	1
229	退回	tuì huí	back to	32
230	退货	tuì huò	to return goods	17
231	外卖	wài mài	take-away food	12
232	网红	wǎng hóng	online celebrity	32

· 177 ·

续 表

序 号	词 语	拼 音	翻 译	课
233	网上购物	wǎng shàng gòu wù	online shopping	16
234	网速	wǎng sù	network speed	29
235	往返	wǎng fǎn	round trip	23
236	往前	wǎng qián	forward	1
237	微信	wēi xìn	WeChat	10
238	微信名片	wēi xìn míng piàn	WeChat business card	31
239	微信群	wēi xìn qún	WeChat group	31
240	卫生间	wèi shēng jiān	toilet	28
241	卧铺	wò pù	sleeper	22
242	卧室	wò shì	bedroom	28
243	无线网络	wú xiàn wǎng luò	wireless network	29
244	无座	wú zuò	no seat	22
245	物流信息	wù liú	the logistics information	16
246	西瓜汁	xī guā zhī	watermelon juice	8
247	西红柿炒鸡蛋	xī hóng shì chǎo jī dàn	scrambled egg with tomato	7
248	喜剧演员	xǐ jù yǎn yuán	comedian	26
249	下午	xià wǔ	afternoon	2
250	现金	xiàn jīn	cash	10
251	线路图	xiàn lù tú	circuit diagram	21
252	写作课	xiě zuò kè	writing course	3
253	新鲜	xīn xiān	fresh	13
254	信息采集	xìn xī cǎi jí	information acquisition	27
255	行程表	xíng chéng biǎo	schedule	20
256	型号	xíng hào	model	17

续表

序号	词语	拼音	翻译	课
257	押金	yā jīn	deposit	28
258	严格	yán gé	strict	3
259	验血	yàn xiě	a blood test	30
260	羊肉	yáng ròu	mutton	13
261	药房	yào fáng	pharmacy	30
262	一等座	yī děng zuò	first class	22
263	一共	yí gòng	a total of	13
264	一直	yì zhí	straight forward	1
265	医疗指南	yī liáo zhǐ nán	medical guide	30
266	英镑	yīng bàng	pound	27
267	营业厅	yíng yè tīng	business hall	29
268	硬座	yìng zuò	hard seat	22
269	优惠广告	yōu huì guǎng gào	preferential AD	14
270	优惠套餐	yōu huì tào cān	discount package	29
271	邮费	yóu fèi	postage	17
272	右拐	yòu guǎi	turn right	1
273	鱼香肉丝	yú xiāng ròu sī	shredded pork in fish-flavored sauce	7
274	语音电话	yǔ yīn diàn huà	voice call	31
275	浴缸	yù gāng	bathtub	25
276	预订	yù dìng	booking	23/24
277	预留	yù liú	reserved	24
278	元	yuán	*yuan*	13
279	元宵	yuán xiāo	glutinous rice ball for Lantern Festival	33
280	元宵节	yuán xiāo jié	Lantern Festival	6

续 表

序 号	词 语	拼 音	翻 译	课
281	原创	yuán chuàng	originality	32
282	原价	yuán jià	original price	15
283	月饼	yuè bing	moon cake	6
284	阅读课	yuè dú kè	reading course	3
285	暂停	zàn tíng	suspended	32
286	早餐券	zǎo cān quàn	breakfast voucher	25
287	怎么样	zěn me yàng	How's that	5
288	炸鸡	zhá jī	fried chicken	12
289	站	zhàn	station	19
290	站台	zhàn tái	platform	21
291	账单	zhàng dān	bill	27
292	账号	zhàng hào	account number	27
293	整租	zhěng zū	whole rent	28
294	支付	zhī fù	pay	20
295	支付宝	zhī fù bǎo	Alipay	10
296	质量	zhì liàng	quality	17
297	中秋节	zhōng qiū jié	Mid-Autumn Festival	6
298	重阳节	chóng yáng jié	Double Ninth Festival	6
299	周二	zhōu èr	Tuesday	5
300	猪肉	zhū ròu	pork	13
301	转账	zhuǎn zhàng	transfer	27
302	自动售票机	zì dòng shòu piào jī	automatic ticket machine	21
303	自付	zì fù	self-pay	17
304	综合课	zōng hé kè	comprehensive course	3

续表

序号	词语	拼音	翻译	课
305	粽子	zòng zi	Zongzi	6
312	最近	zuì jìn	recently	3
313	座位	zuò wèi	seat	26
314	做东	zuò dōng	to play the host	10